# Portra[it] of Christ in the Tabernacle

by **Theodore H. Epp**
Director
Back to the Bible Broadcast

A
**BACK TO THE BIBLE
PUBLICATION**

**Back to the Bible**
Lincoln, Nebraska 68501

85,000 printed to date—1976
(5-5506—85M—106)
ISBN 0-8474-1233-4

Printed in the United States of America

# Foreword

The Old Testament tabernacle provides many parallels to New Testament truths. In particular, it emphasizes the one way of salvation—through shedding of blood—and the need to worship and fellowship with God.

In *Portraits of Christ in the Tabernacle*, Theodore H. Epp searches out the fine shades of meaning of the tabernacle and relates them to salvation and the believer's daily walk. The Christian life becomes even richer in meaning as it is compared with the tabernacle.

As an aid to study, charts of the tabernacle appear on pages 6 and 7. These charts should be referred to often as the study progresses from one position in the tabernacle to another, and from one piece of furniture to another.

May the God who came to dwell among men in the tabernacle, and later in the person of Jesus Christ, enable you to glean many spiritual riches from this book.

—Harold J. Berry
Personal Assistant
to Theodore H. Epp

# Contents

**Chapter**                                        **Page**

1. Portraits of Christ in the Tabernacle . . . . 9
2. Names Given to the Tabernacle . . . . . 23
3. Location, Materials and Their Significance . . 33
4. The Purposes of the Tabernacle . . . . . 45
5. God Makes the First Move . . . . . . 51
6. The Fence and the Gate . . . . . . 57
7. The Altar and the Laver . . . . . . . 67
8. The Tabernacle Building . . . . . . . 85
9. The Door to the Holy Place . . . . . . 99
10. The Table of Showbread . . . . . . .103
11. The Golden Lampstand . . . . . . .113
12. The Golden Altar . . . . . . . . .125
13. The Holy of Holies . . . . . . . .131
14. The Veil . . . . . . . . . . .145
15. A Pattern for the Devotional Time . . . .153

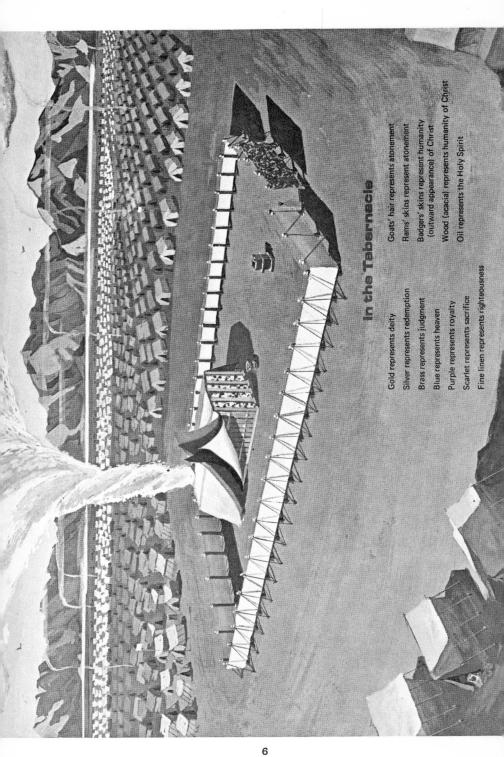

## In the Tabernacle

Gold represents deity

Silver represents redemption

Brass represents judgment

Blue represents heaven

Purple represents royalty

Scarlet represents sacrifice

Fine linen represents righteousness

Goats' hair represents atonement

Rams' skins represent atonement

Badgers' skins represent humanity
(outward appearance) of Christ

Wood (acacia) represents humanity of Christ

Oil represents the Holy Spirit

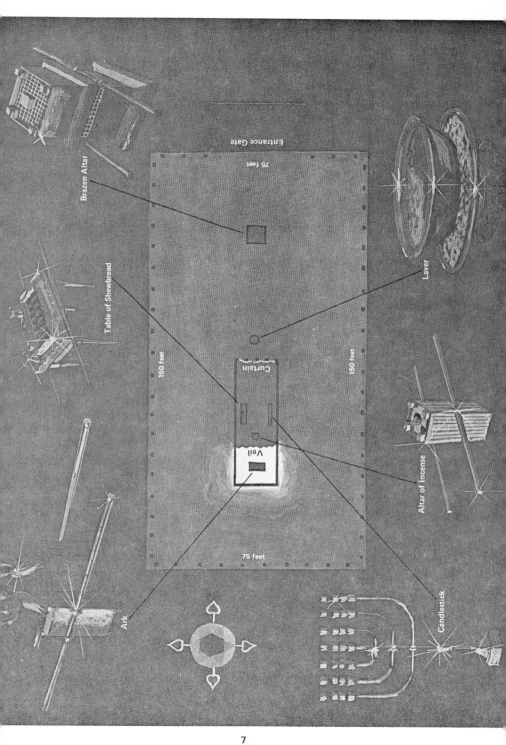

Brazen Altar

Table of Shewbread

Laver

Altar of Incense

Ark

Candlestick

Entrance Gate

75 feet

150 feet

150 feet

75 feet

Curtain

Veil

7

# Chapter 1

# Portraits of Christ in the Tabernacle

After God had delivered Israel from Egypt by means of the shed blood of the sacrificial lamb (Ex. 12), the Israelites journeyed to the southern tip of the Sinai peninsula. They stopped at Mount Sinai, where their leader, Moses, received the Law and instructions concerning the tabernacle from God.

## God Seeks Man

The purpose of the tabernacle was to allow God to dwell among the Israelites in order to meet their needs. God told Moses: "Let them [the Israelites] make me a sanctuary; that I may dwell among them. According to all that I shew thee, after the pattern of the tabernacle, and the pattern of all the instruments thereof, even so shall ye make it" (Ex. 25:8,9).

God's compassion for His people was evident in that He wanted to dwell among them. Although God expresses wrath toward sin, He is a God of love and wants fellowship with those who place their faith in Him.

Notice that it was God who wanted to dwell with the people. Even though they did not necessarily seek God, He sought them. This is the way God has worked since the beginning of time. When Adam and Eve chose to go their own way instead of God's way, bringing about the fall into sin, God made the first move to seek them. After eating the forbidden fruit, "they [Adam and Eve] heard the voice of the Lord God walking in the garden in the cool of the day: and Adam and his wife hid themselves from the presence of the Lord God amongst the trees of the garden. And the Lord

God called unto Adam, and said unto him, Where art thou?" (Gen. 3:8,9). They were not seeking God, but God was seeking them.

God also made the first move to seek man at a later time. Two brothers, Cain and Abel, brought offerings to God. Abel's was accepted, but Cain's was not (see Gen. 4:1-5). Again the Lord made the first move toward man. "The Lord said unto Cain, Why art thou wroth? And why is thy countenance fallen? If thou doest well, shalt thou not be accepted? And if thou doest not well, sin lieth at the door. And unto thee shall be his desire, and thou shalt rule over him" (vv. 6,7). The word translated "sin" can also be translated "sin offering." In essence, God was saying that there was no need for Cain to be angry because a sin offering was available if he would only make it.

However, Cain became so angry with his brother that he eventually murdered him (v. 8). Even after this the Lord appeared to Cain and asked about Abel (v. 9). So in this incident, too, we observe that God made the first move to seek fellowship with man.

This same principle is also seen in the New Testament. Concerning Jesus Christ, the Bible says, "He came unto his own, and his own received him not. But as many as received him, to them gave he power to become the sons of God, even to them that believe on his name: which were born, not of blood, nor of the will of the flesh, nor of the will of man, but of God" (John 1:11-13).

Jesus came to earth to live among men and to die on the cross for the sin of the world. At the Last Supper He told His disciples: "Let not your heart be troubled: ye believe in God, believe also in me. In my Father's house are many mansions: if it were not so, I would have told you. I go to prepare a place for you. And if I go and prepare a place for you, I will come again, and receive you unto myself; that where I am, there ye may be also" (14:1-3). So again the principle that God seeks man is seen.

## Three Compartments

As God met Moses on Mount Sinai and described to him how the tabernacle should be built, He began with the ark of the covenant, which was to be placed in the Holy of Holies, and concluded with the altar of sacrifice in the outer court. (See the chart on page 7 for the arrangement of the tabernacle furniture.) There were three compartments to the tabernacle: the Holy of Holies, the Holy Place and the outer court. It is common for us to think of these compartments in reverse order; that is, the outer court, the Holy Place, and the Holy of Holies. This was the way a person approached God. However, God began His description of the tabernacle with the ark, which was to be the place of His abode. Then He worked outward toward the outer court. God did not first begin with the sinner but with the place of His abode where forgiveness and mercy could be obtained.

The ark of the covenant in the Holy of Holies and the altar in the outer court represent two extremes. The ark of the covenant was the place where justice and judgment were established. Because God is sinless, He is absolutely just and must judge against sin. On the other hand, the altar of sacrifice in the outer court was the place where the sinner first came to meet God in mercy and truth. These thoughts will be developed in more detail as the study continues.

Man did not directly approach God by immediately coming to the ark of the covenant. As noted earlier, God first approaches man, and He did this by meeting man at the altar of sacrifice in the outer court. The sinner could not have faced God's justice and judgment without experiencing death, but mercy and truth could bring God out to the sinner. Because of God's absolute justice, no sinner could be admitted directly into His presence. There first had to be a sacrifice for sin, and this was accomplished at the altar. This sacrifice allowed God to meet man in mercy and truth; thus, the sacrifice brought God out to the sinner.

God's purpose in the tabernacle was to dwell among men and to meet their needs. In this we find a portrait of Christ—He, too, came to earth to fulfill God's plan of meeting man's need. The Lord Jesus Christ traveled from God's throne to Calvary's cross to meet man's need. After dying on the cross to pay the penalty for sin, Jesus returned to the Heavenly Father (see Phil. 2:5-11). Christ traveled from glory to shame and then went from shame back to glory. In Christ, God comes in perfect grace to meet the sinner. And in Christ, the sinner is brought in perfect righteousness to meet God. This is God's wonderful plan.

As we consider the portrait of Christ seen in the tabernacle, it is evident that the way from the ark to the brazen altar was marked with love, and the way from the altar to the ark of God was sprinkled with the blood of atonement. Because of His love God sent His only Son to earth to pay the penalty for sin (see John 3:16). Only by faith in Him are the benefits of His shed blood applied to a person. The one who believes in Jesus Christ as personal Saviour receives forgiveness of sins and everlasting life.

### God's High Standards

The high standards of God are apparent in the tabernacle. The demands of God must be met or else there is no forgiveness. God is absolutely holy and cannot lower His standards in any way. The Ten Commandments, which contained God's holy demands, were placed within the ark of the covenant in the Holy of Holies. But no one is able to keep the Law perfectly, so the only hope is to rely on the sacrifice for sin. God's righteous demands were met by Christ's sacrifice on the cross for the sin of the world. The Bible says, "He is the propitiation [satisfaction] for our sins: and not for our's only, but also for the sins of the whole world" (I John 2:2). The purpose of the Law was to show man how far short he had come of the holy standards of God so he would place faith in Jesus Christ as his Saviour.

Aaron's rod that budded was also in the ark of the covenant. Aaron was a priest who mediated between God and man, and in this sense he represented Jesus Christ, who is our High Priest. The Bible says, "For there is one God, and one mediator between God and men, the man Christ Jesus" (I Tim. 2:5).

Also in the ark was a pot of manna—the miracle food God provided Israel in the wilderness. This was a constant reminder that spiritual nourishment comes only from God.

The ark of the covenant was overshadowed by the mercy seat. This mercy seat was the place where God dwelt among men. The mercy seat will be examined in detail later, but it is mentioned at this point to emphasize that God is a God of mercy as well as a God of judgment. Only because God is a God of mercy did He permit men's sins to be taken care of by another.

For man to enter God's presence with sin would contaminate God's holiness, but man was allowed to approach God on the basis of the sprinkled blood. So also, Jesus Christ paid the penalty for all sin and became the sacrifice which satisfied the holy demands of God. By means of the sacrifice of Christ, God was able to maintain His righteous standards while delivering everyone who believed in Jesus Christ from condemnation. Romans 3:26 expresses this point: "That he might be just, and the justifier of him which believeth in Jesus."

### Parallels to the Individual

Another parallel seen in the tabernacle—it had three distinct parts just as every person does. The tabernacle was comprised of the outer court, the Holy Place, and the Holy of Holies. Every person is comprised of body, soul and spirit. Many interesting parallels can be drawn between the tabernacle and an individual, especially a Christian.

The outer court of the tabernacle compares to a person's body—it is visible to the world. The Holy Place and the Holy of Holies were covered, but the outer court was exposed to the world. Similarly, a person's body is all that is visible to the world; the real person lives within the body. Since it is a person's body that comes into contact with the world, the body is often referred to as the world-conscious part of man.

The tabernacle also contained the Holy Place, which was invisible to the world because it was under coverings. This corresponds to a person's soul, the seat of affections and reasoning capacity. Decision-making takes place in the soul. A person's soul is not visible to the world, but since the individual is intensely aware of what goes on within his soul, it is commonly referred to as that capacity which gives man self-consciousness.

The Holy of Holies was also concealed from world view. This was the seat of God's habitation where communion with God could take place around the mercy seat. The Holy of

Holies corresponds to man's spirit, which gives him a sensitivity to the things of God. A believer's spirit is sometimes referred to as the inner man.

The spirit of man makes him distinctively different from animals. Although they have world-consciousness and self-consciousness, they do not have the capacity to commune with God; they do not have God-consciousness. The spirit of man gives him this capacity.

A person is able to communicate with God only through the capacity of his spirit. God looks into the heart of each person to see the intent of the words he speaks. The voice of the spirit communes with God.

### Parallels to Christ's Words

Parallels can also be seen between the tabernacle and the words of Christ as recorded in John 14:6: "I am the way, the truth, and the life." Consider these words in relationship to the tabernacle.

Jesus said, "I am the way," which corresponds to the outer court where the brazen altar stood. The sacrifices were made on the altar, and it was only by means of sacrifice that one could approach God. Jesus Christ is the way to God, for He is the sacrifice for sin.

Also in the outer court, between the altar and the Holy Place, was the laver. This was simply a tub-like receptacle with water in it. Its purpose was to provide cleansing as the priest came daily in his ministering capacity. It was necessary for the priest to wash his hands and his feet before entering the Holy Place.

So, too, believers are admonished to be clean from contacts with the world after they have come to God by means of the sacrifice of Christ. This is emphasized for the believer in Hebrews 10:19-22: "Having therefore, brethren, boldness to enter into the holiest by the blood of Jesus, by a new and living way, which he hath consecrated for us, through the veil, that is to say, his flesh; and having an high priest over the house of God; let us draw near with a true heart in full assurance of faith, having our hearts sprinkled from an evil conscience, and our bodies washed with pure water."

Christ also said that He is the truth (see John 14:6). Underneath the coverings of the tabernacle were two rooms, the Holy Place and the Holy of Holies. The Holy Place was the larger room, and here the priest entered to worship God in truth. When Christ was on earth, He told the woman of Samaria, "They that worship him [God] must worship him in spirit and in truth" (4:24).

In the Holy Place of the tabernacle, where the priest entered to worship God, was the candlestick, the table of showbread and the altar of incense. Each of these represents the Lord Jesus Christ, for He is the Light of the World, the Bread of Life and the intercessor for all believers.

Jesus also said, "I am . . . the life" (14:6). This corresponds with the Holy of Holies, where the presence of God dwelled. Only there could spiritual life be extended to the Israelites by the high priest propitiating God for the sins of the people. Today, there is no temple on earth where a person must come to approach God. Jesus Christ has paid the penalty for sin, and anyone can receive forgiveness of sins and eternal life by trusting Christ as Saviour. This is only possible, however, because Jesus Christ has completely satisfied the holy demands of God for sin. But having done so, Christ was able to say, "I am . . . the life" (v. 6).

First John 5:11,12 also emphasizes that Jesus Christ is the life: "This is the record, that God hath given to us eternal life, and this life is in his Son. He that hath the Son hath life; and he that hath not the Son of God hath not life."

## Tabernacle Points to Christ

The tabernacle is a type of the Lord Jesus Christ. Everything in the tabernacle points forward to His Person and work.

The tabernacle was the place where God came to meet man, and it represented the one Person in whom deity and humanity met—the Lord Jesus Christ. Every feature of the tabernacle prefigured the Person and work of Christ.

For the nation of Israel, the tabernacle was the center of worship. This was true first in the desert, then in the land, although the temple later took the place of the tabernacle.

The design of the temple was based on the instructions God gave Moses concerning the tabernacle.

As God instructed Moses on Mount Sinai concerning the tabernacle, He said, "According to all that I shew thee, after the pattern of the tabernacle, and the pattern of all the instruments thereof, even so shall ye make it" (Ex. 25:9). The construction of the tabernacle was not left to Moses' imagination; God gave detailed instructions for every aspect of it.

The New Testament Book of Hebrews specifically mentions that Moses built the tabernacle precisely as God instructed: "Moses was admonished of God when he was about to make the tabernacle: for, See, saith he, that thou make all things according to the pattern shewed to thee in the mount" (8:5).

Because the tabernacle foreshadows the Person and work of Christ, it can be said that Christ was the ultimate fulfillment of the tabernacle. John 1:14 seems to draw a parallel between the tabernacle and Christ: "The Word was made flesh, and dwelt among us, (and we beheld his glory, the glory as of the only begotten of the Father,) full of grace and truth." The Greek word translated "dwelt" in this verse literally means "tabernacled." That Christ tabernacled among men is a direct parallel to the purpose of God in the Old Testament tabernacle: "Let them make me a sanctuary; that I may dwell among them" (Ex. 25:8). Thus, the Old Testament tabernacle, which permitted God to dwell among the people, prefigured the time when Jesus Christ would take upon Himself a human body and tabernacle among men. Christ provided the all-sufficient and perfect provision for total redemption.

### A Picture of the Believer

The tabernacle, in a secondary manner, also pictures the believer. Jesus Christ tabernacled among men, but because the believer is in Christ, he dwells, or tabernacles, in God. Jesus was the tabernacle in whom dwelt all the fullness of the Godhead bodily (see Col. 2:9,10), and the believer positionally dwells in Christ. Believers are told: "For by one Spirit are we all baptized into one body, whether we be Jews or Gentiles, whether we be bond or free; and have been all made to drink into one Spirit" (I Cor. 12:13). Ephesians 1:22,23 specifically reveals that Christ is the Head of the body: "[God] hath put all things under his feet, and gave him to be the head over all things to the church, which is his body, the fulness of him that filleth all in all." The Scriptures use the tabernacle, and its later counterpart the temple, to illustrate how believers are joined together. Concerning the position believers have in Christ, Paul said, "In whom all the building fitly framed together groweth unto an holy temple in the Lord: in whom ye also are builded together for an habitation of God through the Spirit" (2:21,22).

So while the tabernacle foreshadows the Person and work of Christ, it also illustrates the believer, who dwells in Christ and is himself indwelt by Christ. The Bible tells believers: "Christ in you, the hope of glory" (Col. 1:27).

## A Picture of God's Salvation

The tabernacle also gives a complete picture of God's plan of salvation. It emphasizes every aspect of salvation, from salvation from the guilt of sin to the believer's perfect rest and peace in Christ's presence. These aspects of salvation as seen in the tabernacle will be discussed in detail later.

As already mentioned, various coverings concealed the Holy Place and the Holy of Holies. One would have an entirely different view of the tabernacle depending on whether he viewed it from the outside or from the inside. These two viewpoints would be in sharp contrast to each other. From the outside, the tabernacle was unattractive, but there was breathtaking splendor and beauty on the inside. This also pointed to the Person of Jesus Christ. We do not know precisely what Jesus looked like physically, but that is not nearly as important as who He was inwardly, the God-Man.

The stranger standing outside the tabernacle would see only two things—the white linen fence surrounding the court and the top part and the roof of the building inside the court. The white linen represented Christ's perfect righteousness. On the roof of the building inside the court, the stranger would see only the drab leather curtain of badger skins, bleached by the hot desert sun.

The person outside the tabernacle represents the sinner, or natural man, without Jesus Christ. As the unbeliever views the tabernacle, he sees nothing that especially draws him to it. However, the priest, representative of the believer who has the privilege of going inside by means of the shed blood, sees a glorious beauty. The Old Testament priesthood was limited to a few, but every believer today is a priest—he is able to approach the throne of God directly (see Heb. 4:14-16).

Only those who have trusted Jesus Christ as personal Saviour are able to see the true beauty of Christ.

Although the unbeliever outside the temple and the believer inside the temple both see Christ, how differently they behold Him! The unbeliever outside the temple sees the white linen wall representing Christ's perfect righteousness. Even though the unbeliever may admit that Christ was not an ordinary man and might even admire Christ's ideals and moral character, he does not fully understand the deity of Christ. The unbeliever might even be impressed with the wisdom and teachings of Christ, but doctrines such as the virgin birth of Christ would probably be foolishness to him. The unbeliever fails to see the value of the atonement, the validity of the resurrection of Christ, and the reality of His coming again. To an unbeliever Christ, at most, is a great man. He has no capacity to really appreciate the beauty of Christ's inner man.

Until a person is born again, he sees nothing more in Christ than His perfect humanity and moral perfection. The unbeliever might think that Christ was noble in His life and that He died a martyr's death, but he is not able to grasp why He really died—to pay the penalty of sin for the unbeliever.

Isaiah prophesied the way the world would look on Christ: "He hath no form nor comeliness; and when we shall see him, there is no beauty that we should desire him" (Isa. 53:2). For those who look only on the external, there is nothing about Christ that causes them to want to be in right relationship with Him. The Bible states why the true beauty of Jesus Christ is not appreciated by an unbeliever: "The natural man receiveth not the things of the Spirit of God: for they are foolishness unto him: neither can he know them, because they are spiritually discerned" (I Cor. 2:14).

The unbeliever also often scoffs at what Jesus Christ accomplished on the cross for the world, "for the preaching of the cross is to them that perish foolishness; but unto us which are saved it is the power of God" (1:18). The Apostle Paul said, "If our gospel be hid, it is hid to them that are lost: in whom the god of this world hath blinded the minds of them which believe not, lest the light of the glorious gospel of Christ, who is the image of God, should shine unto them" (II Cor. 4:3,4). Notice who says it is "the glorious gospel of Christ"—only that person who has trusted Jesus Christ and is, therefore, on the inside.

The person on the outside views Christ as only a martyr, but the believer, who is on the inside, realizes the truth of Philippians 2:6-8: "Who, although He existed in the form of God, did not regard equality with God a thing to be grasped, but emptied Himself, taking the form of a bondservant, and being made in the likeness of men. And being found in appearance as a man, He humbled Himself by becoming obedient to the point of death, even death on a cross" (NASB).

### Personal Application

How about you? Have you entered the tabernacle to see the real beauty of Christ; that is, have you recognized that you are a sinner and that only Christ has paid the penalty for your sin? If you have recognized that, have you placed your trust in Jesus Christ as your Saviour from condemnation? One may enter the tabernacle to behold its beauty and glory only one way, by means of the altar. One can come into right relationship with God by only one way—by placing faith in Jesus Christ, who shed His blood on the cross to pay the penalty of sin.

The Lord Jesus Christ Himself said, "He that entereth not by the door into the sheepfold, but climbeth up some other way, the same is a thief and a robber. . . . I am the door: by me if any man enter in, he shall be saved, and shall go in and out, and find pasture. The thief cometh not, but for to steal, and to kill, and to destroy: I am come that they might have life, and that they might have it more abundantly" (John 10:1,9,10). No wonder Christ said, "I am the way, the truth, and the life: no man cometh unto the Father, but by me" (14:6).

The sinner, entering the tabernacle by the gate, came face to face with the altar of burnt offerings—a perfect picture of the cross of Jesus Christ. Because there was only one way to enter, the tabernacle was both exclusive and inclusive. It excluded all who would not come the one and only way, but it included all who came the prescribed way. Just as it shut out all who refused to come the one way, so it shut in with God and gave true safety to those who came the proper way. The security of believers who come by the one way of salvation is a reminder of Jesus' words: "My sheep hear my voice, and I know them, and they follow me: and I give unto them eternal life; and they shall never perish, neither shall any man pluck them out of my hand. My Father, which gave them me, is greater than all; and no man is able to pluck them out of my Father's hand" (10:27-29).

The manner in which the tabernacle excluded some and included others is also a reminder of what happened when Noah built the ark to escape the worldwide flood. After the animals and Noah and his family had entered the ark, "the Lord shut him in" (Gen. 7:16). This single act of the Lord not only shut Noah into the ark, but it also shut out all those who had refused to come by faith.

Also, on Mount Sinai God gave Moses two things to show that some were shut out and that others were shut in. The Law which God gave Moses revealed man's awful sin and desperate failure and showed that he was excluded from God. However, the tabernacle revealed God's way of mercy for the guilty sinner who would come by faith and be shut in to God.

First, God gave the Law to show His holy and just demands and the penalty of condemnation and death. Then, He gave the tabernacle to reveal His mercy and the way of forgiveness and perfect salvation. It was provided for all who would admit they were hopelessly lost and could not save themselves and who, therefore, came His provided way.

This is a reminder of Romans 8:3: "For what the law could not do, in that it was weak through the flesh, God sending his own Son in the likeness of sinful flesh, and for sin, condemned sin in the flesh."

Chapter 2

# Names Given to the Tabernacle

Throughout this study the structure God instructed Moses to build is referred to as "the tabernacle." However, several other names were used in referring to it. In all, seven names were given to this structure which so clearly prefigured the Person and work of the Lord Jesus Christ.

The names given to the tabernacle reveal the importance the Israelites attached to the tabernacle. To know how they referred to it is to better understand its significance in their national life as a people of God.

## Tent

The tabernacle is frequently referred to as the tent (Ex. 39:32,33,40). A tent is an outer covering, and because it is something movable it suggests a pilgrimage. A tent is a temporary place of dwelling; it is not permanent.

God intended for the tabernacle to be temporary so that it could be set up and taken down whenever He wanted the people to camp or move on to another site. But it was also to be temporary because it was primarily designed for the wilderness, and God wanted them to keep moving toward the Promised Land.

So also, the Church, which is the Body of Christ, is temporarily on earth, but its ultimate goal is the New Jerusalem (see Rev. 21, 22). The Body of Christ is composed of every person who has trusted Jesus Christ as Saviour during this Church Age. Each believer serves Jesus Christ on earth now, but he will eventually be a part of the New Jerusalem.

The believer's body is also temporary. Although the person who has trusted Jesus Christ as Saviour has eternal life, his body will someday experience death, unless the Lord Jesus Christ returns first to catch away believers to heaven. But when the Christian experiences physical death, the real person—the soul and the spirit—go directly to be with the Lord. The Scriptures indicate that when a believer is absent from the body, he is present with the Lord (see II Cor. 5:8).

Concerning the believer's body, II Corinthians 5:1 says, "For we know that if our earthly house of this tabernacle were dissolved, we have a building of God, an house not made with hands, eternal in the heavens." While the believer is on earth, his body is like a tent-house; he inhabits it only while waiting for his permanent residence in heaven. How wonderful to realize that every believer has a building of God prepared for him in heaven, which will be his permanent dwelling for all eternity.

Here on earth we look at an individual and say, "There goes Mr. Smith." However, we are only looking at the tabernacle he dwells in. If he is a believer, he will someday have a permanent dwelling. The more difficulties a believer experiences with his body in this life, the more he looks forward to receiving the new body God has prepared for him. This is what Paul referred to when he said, "For in this we groan, earnestly desiring to be clothed upon with our house which is from heaven" (v. 2).

By considering the tent as a temporary dwelling, one can better understand the life of Abraham. Although he was probably one of the wealthiest men of his time, he lived in a tent rather than a mansion. Hebrews 11:9,10 says concerning Abraham: "By faith he lived as an alien in the land of promise, as in a foreign land, dwelling in tents with Isaac and Jacob, fellow-heirs of the same promise; for he was looking for the city which has foundations, whose architect and builder is God" (NASB). Abraham's confidence was not in the things of this world but in the God he served.

If you know Jesus Christ as your Saviour, what is your attitude toward the place in which you live? Do you view it, as well as your other possessions, as temporary blessings to help you serve God, or do you feel as if you will live there forever? Is your confidence in the things of this world or in eternal values?

The word "tent" was also used to refer to the tabernacle as a meeting place (see Ex. 36:14). The tabernacle was the meeting place of God and men. In fact, it was the only place where God and man could meet on the basis of the shed blood of the sacrifices.

When God told Moses to build the tabernacle, He said, "There I will meet with thee, and I will commune with thee" (25:22). Thus, a key purpose of the tabernacle was to enable God to meet and commune with His own as they came by the prescribed way of the sacrifices.

The believer today is able to approach God on the basis of the shed blood of Jesus Christ. No one can approach God in his own merits, but Jesus Christ has opened the way to God for all who believe in His finished work of redemption. This is emphasized in Hebrews 10:19-22: "Since therefore, brethren, we have confidence to enter the holy place by the blood of Jesus, by a new and living way which He inaugurated for us through the veil, that is, His flesh, and since we have a great priest over the house of God, let us draw near with a sincere heart in full assurance of faith, having our hearts sprinkled clean from an evil conscience and our body washed with pure water" (NASB).

### Sanctuary

Another name given to the tabernacle was "sanctuary." God first used this name when He told Moses, "Let them make me a sanctuary; that I may dwell among them" (Ex. 25:8).

The sanctuary was a place set apart for the dwelling of God among men. God said, "I will dwell among the children of Israel, and will be their God. And they shall know that I am the Lord their God, that brought them forth out of the land of Egypt, that I may dwell among them: I am the Lord their God" (29:45,46).

The universal Church is also, in a sense, God's sanctuary. The universal Church refers to those anywhere in the world who have trusted Jesus Christ as personal Saviour. All these are a part of the Body of Christ, known as the Church (see Eph. 1:22,23).

Because the life of Christ is in the Church, which is His Body, the Church is spoken of as a temple. Ephesians 2:19-22 says, "Now therefore ye are no more strangers and foreigners, but fellowcitizens with the saints, and of the household of God; and are built upon the foundation of the apostles and prophets, Jesus Christ himself being the chief corner stone; in whom all the building fitly framed together groweth unto an holy temple in the Lord: in whom ye also are builded together for an habitation of God through the Spirit."

Believers are also asked as a Church, "Know ye not that ye are the temple of God, and that the Spirit of God dwelleth in you? If any man defile the temple of God, him shall God destroy; for the temple of God is holy, which temple ye are" (I Cor. 3:16,17).

The universal Church is also told: "What agreement hath the temple of God with idols? For ye are the temple of the living God; as God hath said, I will dwell in them, and walk in them; and I will be their God, and they shall be my people" (II Cor. 6:16).

In addition to the universal Church's being a temple of God, each individual believer is referred to as a temple. This is because each believer is indwelt by God Himself. The Apostle Paul asked believers, "Do you not know that your body is a temple of the Holy Spirit who is in you, whom you have from God, and that you are not your own? For you have been bought with a price: therefore glorify God in your body" (I Cor. 6:19,20, NASB). Since the Holy Spirit indwells every believer, each believer's body is a temple. The place of God's residence on earth is no longer a building such as the tabernacle or the Old Testament temple, but He dwells within the individual believer's life. Because we who know Christ as Saviour belong to Him, we are told: "Present your bodies a living sacrifice, holy, acceptable unto God, which is your reasonable service" (Rom. 12:1).

### Tabernacle

The word "tabernacle" especially emphasizes the dwelling of God among men. From this dwelling place God spoke to Israel through Moses. This is indicated by Leviticus

1:1: "The Lord called unto Moses, and spake unto him out of the tabernacle of the congregation."

Just as God abode in the tabernacle in Old Testament times, He now abides with believers. Jesus said, "If a man love me, he will keep my words: and my Father will love him, and we will come unto him, and make our abode with him" (John 14:23). God's desire to fellowship with believers is seen in Revelation 3:20: "Behold, I stand at the door, and knock: if any man hear my voice, and open the door, I will come in to him, and will sup with him, and he with me."

The dwelling of Christ in the lives of believers was also mentioned in one of the Apostle Paul's prayers: "That Christ may dwell in your hearts by faith" (Eph. 3:17).

How wonderful it will be for believers when they are in the New Jerusalem where God will dwell in their presence. Referring to this time, Revelation 21:3 says, "Behold, the tabernacle of God is with men, and he will dwell with them, and they shall be his people, and God himself shall be with them, and be their God."

### Tabernacle of the Congregation

The tabernacle was also referred to as "the tabernacle of the congregation" (see Ex. 27:21; Lev. 1:1; Num. 1:1; Deut. 31:14 and so on). Notice that it is "of the congregation," which reveals there was only one true congregation which the Lord came to dwell among in Old Testament times. There were not to be divisions within the congregation.

Just as there was one congregation in the Old Testament—Israel—in which God dwelt, so there is only one body today—the Church. While He was still on earth, Christ said, "I will build my church; and the gates of hell shall not prevail against it" (Matt. 16:18).

This statement of Christ did not refer to a local church but to the universal Church comprised of all regenerated persons from Pentecost to the time when believers will be caught up to meet Him. Every person who trusts Jesus Christ as Saviour is placed into the Body of Christ by the Holy Spirit. The Apostle Paul referred to all believers when he said, "For by one Spirit are we all baptized into one body, whether we be Jews or Gentiles, whether we be bond or free;

and have been all made to drink into one Spirit" (I Cor. 12:13). Notice that it is "one body." Individual believers are members of the Body, but there is only one Body: "Now are they many members, yet but one body" (v. 20).

Again, the Church does not refer to a local congregation or to a denominational group. It refers to all believers, regardless of their religious affiliation. Today, it is sad to see so much divisiveness among believers. One often gets the impression that some denominations think only those within their particular denomination are believers. This is a limited view of the Scriptures and of what God is doing in the lives of His own all around the world.

One of the positive results of various denominations has been the emphasis of various doctrines so that there is not imbalance in any area. Yet so often denominations go to extremes and emphasize a particular doctrine over all others. Regardless of one's denomination or church affiliation, his concern should be to examine the Scriptures and to live on the basis of what they say.

Since the Old Testament tabernacle was a tabernacle of "the" congregation, it is clear that God did not want divisiveness within the congregation. So, too, within the universal Church there should not be divisiveness. The Apostle Paul urged believers to recognize that they are part of one Body and should not be divisive, as if they were serving different purposes. Paul stressed that God had set the members in the Body as it had pleased Him "that there should be no schism in the body; but that the members should have the same care one for another" (I Cor. 12:25).

### Tabernacle of the Lord

The Old Testament tabernacle was also referred to as "the tabernacle of the Lord" (I Kings 2:28). This expression particularly emphasizes that the tabernacle was God's dwelling place; it was not just a place where one went to worship the Lord. It is awesome to realize that God Himself actually dwelled on earth in the tabernacle and that He now dwells on earth in the lives of individual believers. This realization provides not only comfort but also a warning.

Much comfort is to be derived from what the Scriptures say about God's presence with His own. Hebrews 13:5 records the words of Christ: "I will never leave thee, nor forsake thee." What tremendous comfort this promise provides!

Another verse of comfort is Deuteronomy 31:6: "Be strong and of a good courage, fear not, nor be afraid of them: for the Lord thy God, he it is that doth go with thee; he will not fail thee, nor forsake thee." After the death of Moses, God told Joshua, "Have not I commanded thee? Be strong and of a good courage; be not afraid, neither be thou dismayed: for the Lord thy God is with thee whithersoever thou goest" (Josh. 1:9). Today, we can especially be assured that God is with us wherever we go because He indwells every believer (see I Cor. 6:19).

The realization that God dwells with us also provides a warning. This is especially seen in the words of the psalmist as he realized he could not go anyplace to escape the presence of God. The psalmist said, "Whither shall I go from thy spirit? Or whither shall I flee from thy presence? If I ascend up into heaven, thou art there: if I make my bed in hell, behold, thou art there. If I take the wings of the morning, and dwell in the uttermost parts of the sea; even there shall thy hand lead me, and thy right hand shall hold me. If I say, Surely the darkness shall cover me; even the night shall be light about me. Yea, the darkness hideth not from thee; but the night shineth as the day: the darkness and the light are both alike to thee" (Ps. 139:7-12).

So the presence of the tabernacle of the Lord meant that the Lord Himself was among the Israelites. And as we realize that He dwells in each believer, it serves to warn us about the way we live. It is a blessing to know that He is with us, but it is sobering to realize the seriousness of allowing sin to break our fellowship with Him.

Paul emphasized that the individual believer is the tabernacle of the Lord when he said, "I am [have been] crucified with Christ: nevertheless I live; yet not I, but Christ liveth in me" (Gal. 2:20). Paul emphasized the same truth in I Corinthians 6:19 when he said a believer's body is a temple of the Holy Spirit.

## Tabernacle of Testimony

God's dwelling place among men was also known as "the tabernacle of testimony" (Ex. 38:21). Within the ark of the covenant, inside the Holy of Holies, were the Ten Commandments, Aaron's rod that budded and a pot of manna (see Heb. 9:4). These were a testimony of the holiness of God, the need to approach Him the right way, and the sustaining power of God.

The Ten Commandments were especially a testimony of God's righteous standards. These standards could never be lowered, so unless there was a sacrifice to take care of sin, man could never enter God's presence. Having come to God through proper sacrifices, however, the Israelites were to be testimonies in their personal lives of God's righteous standards.

So also, those of us who have placed our faith in Jesus Christ as the Lamb of God who has taken away the sins of the world (see John 1:29) are to be radiant testimonies of His holy standards. Since believers are indwelt by the Holy Spirit, they should reflect to the world the characteristics of God. Each person who knows Christ as Saviour needs to ask himself, What do others see in me?

Jesus told His followers: "Ye are the salt of the earth. . . . Ye are the light of the world" (Matt. 5:13,14). We are to make others thirsty for the things of God. Salt is also a preservative, and as believers have good testimonies before the woi\_d, they are used of God to hold down evil. Who knows the extent that God's judgment is being withheld because a remnant of believers are displaying a good testimony?

We are also to be a light, brilliantly shining forth in the darkness of this world. We must live in such a way that those who become concerned about the things of God will know that they can come to us.

The Bible says that believers are "ambassadors for Christ" (II Cor. 5:20). This means we are His personal representatives to the world. This is an awesome responsibility, and it is important that we reflect the righteous standards of God in the way we live.

Others are watching our lives; they are reading us like

they read a book. Each of us must ask, What are they learning from my life about the Lord Jesus Christ?

Just as the Old Testament tabernacle was a testimony to the surrounding world, so the Church (not its building, but its people) is now to be a testimony. May God give each of us who knows Christ as Saviour wisdom and boldness to live in a way that brings glory to Him and that attracts others to Him.

### Tabernacle of Witness

A seventh name given to the tabernacle was "the tabernacle of witness" (Num. 17:7,8). It was first called this when the rods of the various tribes were placed in the tabernacle to verify which tribe was distinctly chosen to represent God to the others. The next day when Moses went into "the tabernacle of witness; . . . the rod of Aaron for the house of Levi was budded, and brought forth buds, and bloomed blossoms, and yielded almonds" (v. 8).

God instructed Moses to keep Aaron's rod in the tabernacle as a witness that He had invested authority in him (see v. 10).

Believers today are also invested with God's authority. Jesus said, "Ye have not chosen me, but I have chosen you, and ordained you, that ye should go and bring forth fruit, and that your fruit should remain: that whatsoever ye shall ask of the Father in my name, he may give it you" (John 15:16). In other words, if you need anything, just ask the Father for it!

We who know Christ as Saviour are chosen as a royal priesthood to act and speak on the authority of the Lord Jesus Christ. The Bible tells believers: "You also, as living stones, are being built up as a spiritual house for a holy priesthood, to offer up spiritual sacrifices acceptable to God through Jesus Christ" (I Pet. 2:5, NASB). Verse 9 says, "But you are a chosen race, a royal priesthood, a holy nation, a people for God's own possession, that you may proclaim the excellencies of Him who has called you out of darkness into His marvelous light" (NASB). Believers are not called just to say some nice things about the Bible, but they are to speak with the authority of the Lord Jesus Christ because they possess His written Word.

As the tabernacle witnessed to the Old Testament world, we who know Christ today are to witness for Him. Before He ascended to heaven after His resurrection, Jesus said, "You shall receive power when the Holy Spirit has come upon you; and you shall be My witnesses both in Jerusalem, and in all Judea and Samaria, and even to the remotest part of the earth" (Acts 1:8, NASB). He promised that we would be witnesses, but what kind of witnesses are we? Do we know His Word, and do we magnify Him in our daily lives as well as with our words?

Chapter 3

# Location, Materials and Their Significance

Where God chose to place the tabernacle in relationship to the 12 tribes of Israel when they were encamped is highly significant.

## Position of the Tabernacle

It was placed in the center with three tribes camping on each side. The tribe of Levi, from which the priests and tabernacle servants came, camped on the east side near the entrance. The fact that the tabernacle was placed squarely in the center of the tribes reveals that God came to dwell not only among the people but also in the midst of them. With the tabernacle in the center of the camp, there was easy access to it as well as complete protection for all the tribes. The cloud over the tabernacle could spread out over the entire camp so the people would have shade by day and light by night.

God always provides access to Himself as well as protection for His own. Deuteronomy 23:14 says, "For the Lord thy God walketh in the midst of thy camp, to deliver thee, and to give up thine enemies before thee; therefore shall thy camp be holy: that he see no unclean thing in thee, and turn away from thee."

The Psalms also emphasize that God dwells in the midst of His people. Psalm 46:5 says, "God is in the midst of her; she shall not be moved: God shall help her, and that right early."

The New Testament also emphasizes this truth. Referring to the Lord Jesus Christ, Revelation 1:13 says, "In the

33

middle of the lampstands one like a son of man, clothed in a robe reaching to the feet, and girded across His breast with a golden girdle" (NASB). Revelation 2:1 also speaks of God in the midst of His people: "The One who holds the seven stars in His right hand, the One who walks among the seven golden lampstands" (NASB).

These verses reveal that Jesus Christ dwells in the midst of His Church; He is accessible to all who know Him as Saviour.

After the Israelites had completed their wandering in the wilderness, they crossed the Jordan under the leadership of Joshua. Notice especially the function of the ark as the people were crossing. "The priests that bare the ark of the covenant of the Lord stood firm on dry ground in the midst of Jordan, and all of the Israelites passed over on dry ground, until all the people were passed clean over Jordan" (Josh. 3:17). When the priests had, by faith, stepped into the water, the river parted and allowed the people to pass over on dry ground. The priests stood in the riverbed of the Jordan until the people had crossed over. This reveals the protection God gave His people through the ark of the covenant, which was placed in the Holy of Holies when the tabernacle was built.

Christ is not only in the midst of His Church today, He also indwells every believer so that each Christian can say, "Christ liveth in me" (Gal. 2:20). And although we are engaged in spiritual warfare with Satan and his emissaries, we can claim the victory because of what I John 4:4 says: "Greater is he that is in you, than he that is in the world." The Lord Jesus Christ protects His own in every way.

What a wonderful God we have! He not only delivers us from condemnation when we believe in Jesus Christ as Saviour, but He also provides all we need for the daily, spiritual warfare. No wonder the Apostle Paul said, "What shall we say to these things? If God be for us, who can be against us? He that spared not his own Son, but delivered him up for us all, how shall he not with him also freely give us all things? Who shall lay anything to the charge of God's elect? It is God that justifieth. Who is he that condemneth? It is Christ that died, yea rather, that is risen again, who is even at the right hand of God, who also maketh intercession for us" (Rom. 8:31-34).

## Collecting the Materials

A significant amount of the materials were collected by the Israelites when they were in Egypt. Although the Israelites did not know it at the time, they would later need gold, silver and many other items for the tabernacle. But where would they collect these materials in the wilderness? This was taken care of by God, who made sure they had the materials they needed for constructing the tabernacle.

Before the Israelites were delivered from Egypt, God gave instructions concerning their departure. God told Moses, "And I will grant this people favor in the sight of the Egyptians; and it shall be that when you go, you will not go empty-handed. But every woman shall ask of her neighbor and the woman who lives in her house, articles of silver and articles of gold, and clothing; and you will put them on your sons and daughters. Thus you will plunder the Egyptians" (Ex. 3:21,22, NASB).

The Israelites had been serving as slaves to the Egyptians but had not been receiving their pay. What God instructed them to do was essentially to ask for their back wages.

On the night when God passed over the land and killed the firstborn of every family which had not applied blood to the door, the Israelites quickly fled the land. But they remembered to ask for these items as the Lord said they should. "Now the sons of Israel had done according to the word of Moses, for they had requested from the Egyptians articles of silver and articles of gold, and clothing; and the Lord had given the people favor in the sight of the Egyptians, so that they let them have their request. Thus they plundered the Egyptians" (12:35,36, NASB).

So Israel had most of the materials they needed for the tabernacle when God gave instructions to Moses on Mount Sinai concerning its construction. Even though they had these materials, the Israelites were not obligated to give them for the tabernacle, as indicated by the fact that God asked them for a voluntary offering. God told Moses, "Speak unto the children of Israel, that they bring me an offering: of every man that giveth it willingly with his heart ye shall take my offering" (25:2). God had made the Egyptians willing to give the goods to the Israelites, then God asked the Israelites to be willing to give them to Him. It was not that the Israelites were buying God's favor, for He had already displayed His manifold grace to them. Rather, they were to give willingly because of all that God had done for them.

Moses told the Israelites, "This is the thing which the Lord commanded, saying, Take ye from among you an offering unto the Lord: whosoever is of a willing heart, let him bring it, an offering of the Lord; gold, and silver, and brass" (35:4,5). Verse 29 says, "The children of Israel brought a willing offering unto the Lord, every man and woman, whose heart made them willing to bring for all manner of work, which the Lord had commanded to be made by the hand of Moses."

Each morning, Moses brought the voluntary offerings of the people to the workers (see 36:3). Finally, they told Moses, "The people bring much more than enough for the service of the work, which the Lord commanded to make" (v. 5). Think of it! The people were so responsive to God that they gave much more than was needed.

Since the giving did not stop, "Moses gave commandment, and they caused it to be proclaimed throughout the camp, saying, Let neither man nor woman make any more work for the offering of the sanctuary. So the people were restrained from bringing. For the stuff they had was sufficient for all the work to make it, and too much" (vv. 6,7).

Such unusual giving! How wonderful it would be to hear of such giving today. There are instances when more is given for a particular aspect of the Lord's work than is needed, but this is rare. God does not want us to give because we think we must give. We do not give of our substance to pay God back. We are to give out of love so that His work can be furthered (see II Cor. 5:14).

### Lessons in Giving

The New Testament specifically instructs concerning giving. It points out that Jesus Christ gave His all: "For ye know the grace of our Lord Jesus Christ, that, though he was rich, yet for your sakes he became poor, that ye through his poverty might be rich" (II Cor. 8:9). Because we realize all that Christ did for us, we should gladly give out of love for Him.

Concerning giving, believers are told, "But this I say, He which soweth sparingly shall reap also sparingly; and he which soweth bountifully shall reap also bountifully. Every man according as he purposeth in his heart, so let him give; not grudgingly, or of necessity: for God loveth a cheerful giver. And God is able to make all grace abound toward you; that ye, always having all sufficiency in all things, may abound to every good work" (9:6-8).

The Bible speaks of the responsibility of the one who has received spiritual help to give to the one who has helped him. Galatians 6:6 reveals this responsibility: "Let the one who is taught the word share all good things with him who teaches" (NASB). This is a God-given responsibility, and the passage goes on to say, "Do not be deceived, God is not mocked; for whatever a man sows, this he will also reap. For the one who sows to his own flesh shall from the flesh reap corruption, but the one who sows to the Spirit shall from the Spirit reap eternal life" (vv. 6,7, NASB).

It is common for believers to be exceedingly concerned about daily provisions, but Jesus said, "Seek ye first the kingdom of God, and his righteousness; and all these things shall be added unto you" (Matt. 6:33).

A wonderful lesson in giving is also recorded in Proverbs 11:24,25: "There is that scattereth, and yet increaseth; and there is that withholdeth more than is meet, but it tendeth to poverty. The liberal soul shall be made fat: and he that watereth shall be watered also himself."

An understanding of the scriptural teaching about giving eliminates many of today's methods of raising money. People are to voluntarily give as God lays a burden on their hearts. Above all, they need to first give their lives to the Lord in an unrestricted way.

The Scriptures state a principle that is basic to all giving, and unless it is heeded, the giving will not please God. Paul stated this principle when he urged the Corinthians to receive an offering for the poor people in Jerusalem. Paul told the Corinthians that the churches in Macedonia had given abundantly, even out of their deep poverty (II Cor. 8:1-5). Then Paul stated this basic principle for giving: "And this they did, not as we hoped, but first gave their own selves to the Lord, and unto us by the will of God" (v. 5). No giving is pleasing to the Lord until the persons involved have first given themselves.

The importance of a believer's giving himself to the Lord is seen in Romans 12:1: "I beseech you therefore, brethren, by the mercies of God, that ye present your bodies a living sacrifice, holy, acceptable unto God, which is your reasonable service."

Notice the word "therefore" in Romans 12:1. It refers to what has preceded. The three preceding chapters tell of God's relationship with Israel and the wonderful things He has planned for the nation. At the end of chapter 11, Paul broke into a doxology that every believer can identify with: "How fathomless the depths of God's resources, wisdom, and knowledge! How unsearchable His decisions, and how mysterious His methods! For who has ever understood the thoughts of the Lord, or has ever been His adviser? Or who has ever advanced God anything to have Him pay him back? For from Him everything comes, through Him everything lives, and for Him everything exists. Glory to Him forever! Amen" (vv. 33-36, Williams).

No wonder Paul followed these statements with: "I beseech you therefore, brethren" (12:1). Because we have such a great God, the least we can do is present our bodies—which involves all we are—to Him.

We who have trusted Jesus Christ as Saviour are to put ourselves at His disposal because we belong entirely to Him. This truth is emphasized in I Corinthians 6:19,20: "What? Know ye not that your body is the temple of the Holy Ghost which is in you, which ye have of God, and ye are not your own? For ye are bought with a price: therefore glorify God in your body, and in your spirit, which are God's." God has bought us that He might indwell us, just as He indwelt the Old Testament tabernacle. The only way others have of seeing God today is to see Him revealed in believers. But what do they really see in us? Do they see Christ in us? Or do they see only a cantankerous Christian? Having presented our bodies to Him, we are to let Him reflect His own life through us. As Colossians 1:27 says, "Christ in you, the hope of glory."

## According to Pattern

As God instructed Moses concerning the tabernacle, He said, "According to all that I shew thee, after the pattern of the tabernacle, and the pattern of all the instruments thereof, even so shall ye make it" (Ex. 25:9).

Referring to the Old Testament tabernacle and to the priests, Hebrews 8:5 says, "Who serve unto the example and shadow of heavenly things, as Moses was admonished of God when he was about to make the tabernacle: for, See, saith he, that thou make all things according to the pattern shewed to thee in the mount."

Hebrews 9:23 makes a similar statement: "It was therefore necessary that the pattern of things in the heavens should be purified with these; but the heavenly things themselves with better sacrifices than these." From this verse we see that the tabernacle was "the patterns of things in the heavens."

Hebrews 9:24 says, "For Christ is not entered into the holy places made with hands, which are the figures of the true; but into heaven itself, now to appear in the presence of God for us." From this verse we learn that the elements of the Old Testament tabernacle were to be "the figures of the true."

The tabernacle was part of the Mosaic Law system, about which Hebrews 10:1 says, "For the law having a shadow of good things to come, and not the very image of the things, can never with those sacrifices which they offered year by year continually make the comers thereunto perfect." Notice especially the phrase "a shadow of good things to come." So the Old Testament tabernacle and its worship prefigured heavenly things and that which is to come. In particular, the tabernacle prefigured God's plan of salvation, His plan for Christian behavior, the way of worship, and the way we progress to maturity.

Concerning salvation, the tabernacle particularly pictures God's coming to dwell among men; thereby, making it possible for men to approach God. No one can approach God on his own merits; he must come by God's prescribed way. On his own, sinful man cannot approach a sinless God. All must come according to God's pattern and, just as in the tabernacle, it cannot be altered. It cannot be altered because the plan is of God not of men. Hebrews 8:2 emphasizes this truth: "A minister of the sanctuary, and of the true tabernacle, which the Lord pitched, and not man." That the Old Testament tabernacle was related to individual salvation is seen from verse 10: "For this is the covenant that I will make with the house of Israel after those days, saith the Lord; I will put my laws into their mind, and write them in their hearts: and I will be to them a God, and they shall be to me a people."

God's unalterable way of salvation is seen in Ephesians 2:8,9: "For by grace are ye saved through faith; and that not of yourselves: it is the gift of God: not of works, lest any man should boast."

That salvation is not by works is also evident from Titus 3:5: "Not by works of righteousness which we have done, but according to his mercy he saved us, by the washing of regeneration, and renewing of the Holy Ghost."

Ephesians 2:10 directly applies to those who have received Jesus Christ as personal Saviour: "For we are his workmanship, created in Christ Jesus unto good works, which God hath before ordained that we should walk in them."

Acts 4:12 also reveals that there is only one way of salvation: "Neither is there salvation in any other: for there is none other name under heaven given among men, whereby we must be saved." This verse directly relates to John 14:6, which records the words of the Lord Jesus Christ: "I am the way, the truth, and the life: no man cometh unto the Father, but by me."

The Old Testament tabernacle was according to God's pattern, not only concerning salvation but also concerning Christian living. God abode in the Holy of Holies of the tabernacle; thus, He met with the people.

Although there is no tabernacle today, Jesus Christ is within every believer to produce fruit through him. Just as there was only one way to approach God in the tabernacle, so there is only one way for believers to produce fruit in their lives. That one way was specified by the Lord Jesus Christ Himself. He told believers, "Abide in me, and I in you. As the branch cannot bear fruit of itself, except it abide in the vine;

no more can ye, except ye abide in me. I am the vine, ye are the branches: he that abideth in me, and I in him, the same bringeth forth much fruit: for without me ye can do nothing" (John 15:4,5). The only way the believer's life can be satisfactory to God is for him to abide in fellowship. The Christian out of fellowship produces no fruit.

The entire tabernacle—structure, furniture and priestly ministry—was a type of the perfect Christ. All had to be according to what God revealed. Failure on the part of Israel to comply to the heavenly pattern and to its ministry placed the people under the curse of God. This was because the tabernacle was an integral part of the Law, which was binding on the Israelites. The principle of Galatians 3:10 specifically applied to them: "As many as are of the works of the law are under the curse: for it is written, Cursed is every one that continueth not in all things which are written in the book of the law to do them." Thus, any deviation from God's pattern in the tabernacle would bring a curse on Israel. Even though we are not living under the law system today, a curse falls on anyone who endeavors to come to God by any way other than Jesus Christ. There is no other way of salvation (see Acts 4:12).

### Materials

Exodus 25:1-7 mentions the materials that were to be used in building the tabernacle: "The Lord spake unto Moses, saying, Speak unto the children of Israel, that they bring me an offering: of every man that giveth it willingly with his heart ye shall take my offering. And this is the offering which ye shall take of them; gold, and silver, and brass, and blue, and purple, and scarlet, and fine linen, and goats' hair, and rams' skins dyed red, and badgers' skins, and shittim wood, oil for the light, spices for anointing oil, and for sweet incense, onyx stones, and stones to be set in the ephod, and in the breastplate."

These materials and even the colors used typified the Lord Jesus Christ. More will be said about each later, but the basic significance about each item is stated below. Remember that, although the items have a basic symbolical meaning, this meaning is not necessarily to be stressed each time the item appears elsewhere in scriptures.

The following is a list of the items and what each represents:

| Item | Represents |
| --- | --- |
| Gold | Deity |
| Silver | Redemption |
| Brass | Judgment |
| Blue | Heavenly nature |
| Purple | Royalty |
| Scarlet | Sacrifice |
| Wood (acacia) | Humanity of Christ |
| Fine linen | Righteousness |
| Oil | Holy Spirit |
| Rams' skins | Atonement |
| Goats' hair | Atonement |
| Badgers' skins | Humanity or outward appearance of Christ |

That the tabernacle points to the Lord Jesus Christ is evident. For example, the deity and humanity of Christ are represented by the fact that the tabernacle was made of two basic materials—wood and gold.

The wood of the tabernacle was shittim wood, which came from the shittah tree. This was a heavy, hard wood with beautiful grain. It was indestructible by insects; thus, it had all of the qualities that would make it ideal for the tabernacle.

Concerning the tabernacle, God told Moses, "Thou shalt make boards for the tabernacle of shittim wood standing up" (Ex. 26:15). The tree from which the shittim wood came grew under the most adverse circumstances in the desert. As such, it beautifully represented Christ, of whom it was prophesied in Isaiah 53:2: "For he shall grow up before him as a tender plant, and as a root out of a dry ground: he hath no form nor comeliness; and when we shall see him, there is no beauty that we should desire him."

God instructed Moses that the boards of the tabernacle should be overlaid with gold (see Ex. 26:29). This is a beautiful symbol of the relationship of the humanity and deity of the Lord Jesus Christ. Both His humanity and deity are referred to many times in the New Testament, especially in the Gospel of John. John said, "In the beginning was the Word, and the Word was with God, and the Word was God" (1:1). The "Word" to whom John referred was the Lord Jesus Christ, as is evident from verse 14: "And the Word was made flesh, and dwelt among us, (and we beheld his glory, the glory as of the only begotten of the Father,) full of grace and truth."

The term "Word" refers to that which expresses or declares. Thus, John said, "No man hath seen God at any time; the only begotten Son, which is in the bosom of the Father, he hath declared him" (v. 18). The word translated "declared" literally means "to lead out." When the Lord Jesus Christ came to earth, He brought into full revelation the Heavenly Father. This is why Jesus could legitimately say, "He that hath seen me hath seen the Father" (14:9).

The incarnation was a mystery. We cannot understand it completely, but we are able to accept it by faith. Concerning Christ, the Bible says, "For it pleased the Father that in him should all fulness dwell" (Col. 1:19). This is why Paul could state: "For in him dwelleth all the fulness of the Godhead bodily" (2:9).

Jesus Christ was the perfect God-Man, who alone could bring God to man and man to God. Only He could bridge the gulf by dying as a man and rising from the dead as the eternal God. What a great God we have!

The perfect joining of God and man in the Person of Jesus Christ was prefigured in the tabernacle with its wood overlaid with gold. The wood was symbolic of His humanity, and the gold was symbolic of His deity.

The Lord Jesus Christ had to take on a human body to be able to die for the world. Referring to Him, Romans 3:25,26 says, "Whom God hath set forth to be a propitiation through faith in his blood, to declare his righteousness for the remission of sins that are past, through the forbearance of God; to declare, I say, at this time his righteousness: that he might be just, and the justifier of him which believeth in Jesus."

The death of Jesus Christ on the cross made it possible for sinful man to be reconciled to God. The Bible tells believers, "And you, that were sometime alienated and enemies in your mind by wicked works, yet now hath he reconciled" (Col. 1:21). God did not need to be reconciled to man, but man needed to be reconciled to God. Because the death of Christ propitiated, or satisfied, the righteous demands of God (see I John 2:2), all who believe in Jesus Christ as Saviour receive forgiveness of sin and eternal life.

What a great privilege—and tremendous responsibility—it is to proclaim the message of reconciliation. Realizing both the privilege and the responsibility, the Apostle Paul said, "And all things are of God, who hath reconciled us to himself by Jesus Christ, and hath given to us the ministry of reconciliation; to wit, that God was in Christ, reconciling the world unto himself, not imputing their trespasses unto them; and hath committed unto us the word of reconciliation. Now then we are ambassadors for Christ, as though God did beseech you by us: we pray you in Christ's stead, be ye reconciled to God" (II Cor. 5:18-20).

Because there is only one way of salvation, as indicated in Acts 4:12, and because we have been entrusted with the proclamation of this truth (see II Cor. 5:18,19), it is imperative that we be faithful to the responsibility of proclaiming the reconciling work of God. Let us who know Christ as Saviour thank Him that someone brought the Good News to us, and let us be faithful in taking it to others. We must not forget our responsibility now to take the message of reconciliation to others.

Chapter 4

# The Purposes of the Tabernacle

When God gave instructions to Moses concerning the tabernacle, He had three distinct purposes in mind for it. By means of the tabernacle, God planned to dwell in the midst of Israel, to teach man the holiness of God and the sinfulness of mankind, and to show sinful man the only way of salvation.

## To Dwell in Their Midst

That the tabernacle provided God with a place to dwell in the midst of Israel is seen from His words to Moses: "Let them make me a sanctuary; that I may dwell among them" (Ex. 25:8). Because of man's sinfulness, God could not dwell in their midst in just any way, so He prescribed the way this could be done.

Throughout the Scriptures progress is seen in the way God revealed Himself to man. First, God walked in the Garden of Eden in the cool of the day and revealed Himself to Adam and Eve (see Gen. 3:8). The indication is that God had a special way and a special place to meet man at that time.

Second, God revealed Himself to Moses in the burning bush. God spoke to Moses from out of the bush (see Ex. 3:4) and gave him instructions concerning delivering Israel from Egypt (vv. 5-12).

Third, after the Israelites had been delivered from Egypt, God revealed Himself to them in a pillar of a cloud (13:21). It was a pillar of cloud by day and a pillar of fire by night (v. 22). The cloud gave them shade in the daytime, and the fire gave them light at night. God provided the cloud and the fire for the Israelites for the entire period of 40 years between Egypt and Canaan.

Fourth, after Moses had completed the tabernacle exactly as God had instructed, God appeared over it in the same cloud. "The cloud of the Lord was upon the tabernacle by day, and fire was on it by night, in the sight of all the house of Israel, throughout all their journeys" (40:38). Before the tabernacle was built, the Israelites were to move only when the cloud moved. And later, when the cloud was upon the tabernacle, they were still to determine their movements by it. "When the cloud was taken up from over the tabernacle, the children of Israel went onward in all their journeys: but if the cloud were not taken up, then they journeyed not till the day that it was taken up" (vv. 36,37). God often spoke to Moses directly from this cloud.

Fifth, God later revealed Himself in the temple built by Solomon. After the temple was finished, Solomon dedicated it to the Lord. The Bible says, "When Solomon had made an end of praying, the fire came down from heaven, and consumed the burnt-offering and the sacrifices; and the glory of the Lord filled the house" (II Chron. 7:1). The account goes on to explain that the priest could not enter the house because of the glory of the Lord (v. 2) and that when the Israelites saw the fire and the glory of God, "they bowed themselves with their faces to the ground upon the pavement, and worshipped, and praised the Lord, saying, For he is good; for his mercy endureth for ever" (v. 3).

Sixth, during the New Testament era God dwelt among men in the Person of Jesus Christ. The Bible says, "God, after He spoke long ago to the fathers in the prophets in many ways, in these last days has spoken to us in His Son, whom He appointed heir of all things, through whom also He made the world. And He is the radiance of His glory and the exact representation of His nature, and upholds all things by the word of His power. When He had made purification of sins, He sat down at the right hand of the Majesty on high" (Heb. 1:1-3, NASB).

After Jesus Christ finished His work on earth, He ascended to the Father and sent the Holy Spirit to indwell every believer (see John 14:17; 16:7). Today, when a person trusts Christ as his personal Saviour, the Holy Spirit is given to him as the earnest, or pledge, of all that God is going to do for the individual (see Eph. 1:14). Because the Holy Spirit lives within every believer, each believer's body is a temple of the Holy Spirit (see I Cor. 6:19). Think of it! The Holy Spirit indwells those who have trusted Jesus Christ as personal Saviour. All that we are belongs to Jesus Christ because He has bought us with His shed blood and has sent the Holy Spirit to live in us.

Although God could cause the rocks to cry out to proclaim the gospel, He has limited Himself to using individuals who have trusted Christ as Saviour. What a tremendous privilege we have! May we be the kind of witnesses that will glorify God.

### To Teach the Holiness of God and Sinfulness of Man

Another purpose of the tabernacle was to instruct the Israelites concerning God's absolute holiness and their total sinfulness. The holiness of God and the sinfulness of man contrast sharply with each other. Their extreme opposition to each other is clearly evident in the tabernacle worship, which we will be considering later.

In the Holy of Holies God was shut in so sinful man could not get to Him. On the other hand, a wall of linen cloth around the tabernacle shut out sinful man.

Man could approach God, but only through a prescribed way—no exceptions were tolerated. The way to God was through the shedding of a sacrificial animal's blood. This was a type of the Lord Jesus Christ, who shed His blood on the cross; thereby, opening the way to God for us. Because of what the Lord Jesus Christ accomplished on the cross, the writer of Hebrews could say, "Having therefore, brethren, boldness to enter into the holiest by the blood of Jesus" (Heb. 10:19).

God's way of salvation was seen first by pattern in the Old Testament tabernacle, then in the temple, and finally in Christ Himself. All emphasized that there is only one way of salvation. All must come by God's prescribed way, or they will not be delivered from condemnation. Jesus said, "I am the way, the truth, and the life: no man cometh unto the Father, but by me" (John 14:6).

No one else except the Lord Jesus Christ can save from condemnation (see Acts 4:12). Salvation is not gained by works, for no one can be saved in this way. The only way of salvation is through belief in Jesus Christ as personal Saviour (see Eph. 2:8,9; Rom. 4:5).

Unless one comes in God's way, he will remain under condemnation. As John 3:18 says, "He that believeth on him is not condemned: but he that believeth not is condemned already, because he hath not believed in the name of the only begotten Son of God." The Bible also says, "He that believeth on the Son hath everlasting life: and he that believeth not the Son shall not see life; but the wrath of God abideth on him" (v. 36).

First John 5:11,12 states, "This is the record, that God hath given to us eternal life, and this life is in his Son. He that hath the Son hath life; and he that hath not the Son of God hath not life." These verses further emphasize that, unless sinful man comes in God's prescribed way, there is no means of salvation. Many people refuse to accept the fact that there is only one way of salvation; thus, they remain in their sins because they will not come God's way.

### To Reveal the One Way of Salvation

A key purpose of the tabernacle was to emphasize to the Israelites that they could approach God in only one way—by means of a blood sacrifice. In this regard the Old Testament tabernacle was a type of the Lord Jesus Christ, who would shed His blood for sin and be the only way of salvation.

Concerning Moses, the Book of Hebrews says, "Moreover he sprinkled with blood both the tabernacle, and all the vessels of the ministry" (9:21). Verse 22 adds this significant statement: "And almost all things are by the law purged with blood; and without shedding of blood is no remission [forgiveness]."

God had told the Israelites, "For the life of the flesh is in the blood: and I have given it to you upon the altar to make an atonement for your souls: for it is the blood that maketh an atonement for the soul" (Lev. 17:11).

After stating that without the shedding of blood is no forgiveness, the Book of Hebrews says, "It was therefore necessary that the patterns of things in the heavens should be purified with these; but the heavenly things themselves with better sacrifices than these. For Christ is not entered into the holy places made with hands, which are the figures of the true; but into heaven itself, now to appear in the presence of God for us" (9:23,24).

The Scriptures emphasize that Christ gave His body in death and shed His blood for sin. Hebrews 10:9 says, "He taketh away the first, that he may establish the second." The first is the tabernacle, which prefigured what Jesus Christ Himself would do. The next verse adds: "By the which will we are sanctified through the offering of the body of Jesus Christ once for all" (v. 10). Although many sacrifices had to be offered in Old Testament times, Jesus' one sacrifice availed for all time: "For by one offering he hath perfected for ever them that are sanctified" (v. 14).

There is complete salvation through the blood of Christ and only through His blood. Because it is the only means of salvation, Satan opposes an emphasis on the blood of Christ and would like to have it eliminated from our vocabulary and our hymnbooks.

The Scriptures reveal all that we have because of the blood of Jesus Christ. We have redemption and forgiveness through His blood: "In whom we have redemption through his blood, the forgiveness of sins, according to the riches of his grace" (Eph. 1:7). We have justification through His blood: "Much more then, being now justified by his blood, we shall be saved from wrath through him" (Rom. 5:9).

We have sanctification through His blood: "By the which will we are sanctified through the offering of the body of Jesus Christ once for all" (Heb. 10:10). We have cleansing through His blood: "The blood of Jesus Christ his Son cleanseth us from all sin" (I John 1:7).

We also have peace through the blood of Christ: "Having made peace through the blood of his cross, by him to reconcile all things unto himself" (Col. 1:20). The victory over Satan that believers will have during the Tribulation period will also be by the blood of Christ: "They overcame him by the blood of the Lamb, and by the word of their testimony; and they loved not their lives unto the death" (Rev. 12:11).

Even now, the power of Satan has been nullified through Christ's shed blood on the cross. Hebrews 2:14 says concerning Christ: "Since then the children share in flesh and blood, He Himself likewise also partook of the same, that through death He might render powerless him who had the power of death, that is, the devil" (NASB).

# Chapter 5

# God Makes the First Move

One significant theme running throughout Scripture is that God first moves in behalf of man; man does not first move toward God. God always makes the first move to offer complete redemption for mankind and fellowship with Himself.

## Old Testament Examples

This is evident from man's earliest days—even in the Garden of Eden. After Adam and Eve had eaten the forbidden fruit, God appeared in the Garden and called out to Adam: "Where art thou?" (Gen. 3:9). After Adam came out of hiding, God dealt with him and Eve concerning sin, and then He promised a coming Redeemer (v. 15). In the meantime, God offered them a substitute, which involved the shedding of blood—"coats of skins" (v. 21). The tabernacle was also a substitute which God gave to Israel as they waited for the coming Redeemer.

God also made the first move in the incident involving Cain and Abel. Both brought sacrifices to the Lord. Abel's was accepted, but Cain's was rejected. Abel brought "of the firstlings of his flock" (4:4), which indicated that the sacrifice made involved the shedding of blood. Cain brought "of the fruit of the ground" (v. 3), which did not involve the shedding of blood. His sacrifice was rejected because it represented his good works.

Cain was angry with God because his sacrifice was rejected. God asked him why he was angry and stated: "If thou doest well, shalt thou not be accepted? And if thou doest not well, sin [sin offering] lieth at the door" (v. 7).

That God had made the first move is implied by the fact that He had instructed them concerning what kind of sacrifice would be acceptable. In addition, God spoke to Cain about his sin before Cain killed his brother.

God also made the first move hundreds of years later when He saw the wickedness of mankind during Noah's time. The Lord said, "My spirit shall not always strive with man, for that he also is flesh: yet his days shall be an hundred and twenty years" (6:3). Even though mankind was so desperately wicked, God still extended another 120 years of grace. He gave every opportunity for people to repent, and because they refused to do so He brought a worldwide flood to destroy all.

God also made the first move when He called Abraham from Ur of the Chaldees and promised him a land, a seed and a blessing (12:1-3). Through Abraham's seed, or descendants, God was going to provide the Saviour for the world in the Person of the Lord Jesus Christ.

God also moved first in delivering His people from Egypt when they were in slavery there. God promised Moses that He was going to use him to deliver the people (see Ex. 3:9-12). When Pharaoh refused to let the people go after various plagues had been brought upon Egypt, "the Lord smote all the firstborn in the land of Egypt, from the firstborn of Pharaoh that sat on his throne unto the firstborn of the captive that was in the dungeon; and all the firstborn of cattle" (12:29). The Israelites were spared, however, because they had followed God's instruction to put the blood of a lamb on their doorposts (v. 7). God told the Israelites, "When I see the blood, I will pass over you" (v. 13). So the Israelites were delivered from judgment by applying the blood just as we are delivered from eternal condemnation through the shed blood of the Lord Jesus Christ.

### New Testament Examples

The New Testament also abounds with references showing that God made the first move in redemption. Galatians 4:4 says, "When the fulness of the time was come,

God sent forth his Son, made of a woman, made under the law." This was a fulfillment of God's eternal plan of redemption. The Redeemer had been promised to Adam and Eve over 4000 years earlier (see Gen. 3:15). There was no way that man could become good enough on his own to meet God's standards. Thus, God had to make the first move, and as Romans 5:8 says, "While we were yet sinners, Christ died for us." Some people want to become Christians, but they want to wait until they consider themselves good enough. However, they must recognize that they are sinners—that is why Christ died for them. When they trust Him as Saviour, they will receive forgiveness of sin and will be given eternal life.

God also made the first move concerning eternal fellowship between Himself and believers. The night before He was crucified, Jesus told the disciples that He was going away but that He would come back to receive them so they could be with Him (see John 14:1-3). Jesus' words apply to every person: "I am the way, the truth, and the life: no man cometh unto the Father, but by me" (v. 6).

God also made the first move concerning the fellowship believers can have with Him right now. His promise and provision for this wonderful fellowship are mentioned in detail in Romans 6—8. This wonderful fellowship is possible only because God made the first move.

The future is full of hope for the believer because God has also made the first move concerning the eternal destiny of every Christian. The Bible promises that Jesus Christ is someday going to come in the clouds, and believers will be caught up to meet Him in the air (see I Thess. 4:13-18). Revelation 21 and 22 also tells of the eternal state where the believer will be in full fellowship with God. What a wonderful God we have! Although all of us inherited a sinful nature from Adam, God made the first move to provide for our salvation and fellowship with Him.

### The Tabernacle Example

The tabernacle also places the emphasis on God first, rather than man. As God instructed Moses concerning the building of the tabernacle, the first item mentioned was the ark in the Holy of Holies (see Ex. 25:10). The ark contained the Law of God, which revealed His holy, demanding standards. But on top of the ark was the mercy seat, which permitted God to extend mercy to the Israelites as they came by His prescribed way: "And thou shalt put the mercy seat above the ark" (v. 21). Later, we will discuss the significance of the fact that the Holy of Holies was sealed off from the rest of the tabernacle by a veil.

Working from the Holy of Holies outward, the next compartment in the tabernacle was the Holy Place (see chart). In the Holy Place were the table of showbread, the candlestick of pure gold and the altar of incense.

The table of showbread was representative of the sustenance we derive through the Lord Jesus Christ. Jesus Himself said, "I am the bread of life" (John 6:35; see v. 48). The golden candlestick was representative of Christ, who said, "I am the light of the world" (9:5). The altar of incense represented the prayers of believers. Revelation 8:4 associates the prayers of the saints with the smoke of the incense: "The smoke of the incense, which came with the prayers of the saints, ascended up before God out of the angel's hand."

The Holy Place was also veiled off from the outer court by a curtain.

In the outer court, as one moved outward from the Holy Place, was the laver, a large bowl of water. The obvious purpose was for cleansing. The laver represented the Bible, the Word of God. Jesus told believers, "Now ye are clean through the word which I have spoken unto you" (John 15:3).

Farther outward toward the edge of the outer court was the brazen altar on which the sacrifice of blood was made. This altar is representative of the sacrifice of Jesus Christ. Hebrews 10:12 says of Him, "After he had offered one sacrifice for sins for ever, sat down on the right hand of God."

The outer court was veiled off from the outside world by a curtain gate. All of the Israelites were invited to come to the tabernacle to offer sacrifice, but they had to come by God's prescribed way—through the east gate of the tabernacle. So, too, the invitation to be saved is extended to all today, but all must come by God's prescribed way—through the shed blood of the Lord Jesus Christ.

In the tabernacle, God made approach to Him possible by blood; that is, by the blood of a sacrificial offering. In effect, this way was made possible with love because God was not obligated to let sinful man enter His presence.

Many New Testament scriptures tell of God's making a way to Himself. Luke 19:10 says, "The Son of man is come to seek and to save that which was lost." John 1:12,13 says, "As many as received him, to them gave he power to become the sons of God, even to them that believe on his name: which were born, not of blood, nor of the will of the flesh, nor of the will of man, but of God."

Jesus assures everyone, "Him that cometh to me I will in no wise cast out" (6:37). Those who have the Son—those who have trusted Him as personal Saviour—are assured of eternal life. Those who do not have the Son are assured that they do not have this life (see I John 5:10-12).

But in spite of all God has done for mankind, many refuse to come to Him. As Jesus said to the religious leaders of His day, "Ye will not come to me, that ye might have life" (John 5:40). But God has promised "that whosoever believeth in him should not perish, but have everlasting life" (3:16).

So this brief review of the way the tabernacle was laid out shows that the direction moved from God to man. From God's viewpoint, the ark in the Holy of Holies was first, and the brazen altar in the outer court was last. However, the order was reversed from man's viewpoint. He had to come to the brazen altar before approaching God.

Consider the direction the Israelites had to take as they stood on the outside of the tabernacle. They were shut out of the outer court by a wall and could enter only through the gate on the east. Once inside the gate, a person was brought face to face with the place of sacrifice, the brazen altar. The priest could not proceed farther without making this sacrifice. Then he proceeded to the laver for cleansing before entering the Holy Place. As he passed through the veil into the Holy Place, he was in the place of fellowship. As has been mentioned, the table of showbread, the golden candlestick and the altar of incense were in the Holy Place.

Beyond the Holy Place behind a veil was the Holy of Holies. It was the holiest place, where God Himself dwelled. The New Testament tells believers that entrance into the holiest place is made possible through the blood of Jesus (see Heb. 10:19).

Only the high priest could enter the Holy of Holies, and he could enter only once a year. But as we view the spiritual progress revealed in the tabernacle, we identify with him as he came to the ark, and we rejoice in the mercy seat. Those who come the prescribed way become participants in God's abundant mercy. Because Christ has met our need for righteousness, we rejoice in the mercies of God. His mercy endures forever!

Having come by the prescribed way of salvation, we can claim Christ's promise: "I am the door: by me if any man enter in, he shall be saved, and shall go in and out, and find pasture" (John 10:9). We go in for fellowship, and we go out for service. But even as we go out, He leads the way. "When he putteth forth his own sheep, he goeth before them" (v. 4). How thankful we can be that God made the first move in providing salvation and fellowship for lost mankind.

# Chapter 6

# The Fence and the Gate

The Israelites first came to the outer court to establish a relationship with God. They entered through the eastern gate, and in the outer court they found the brazen altar and the laver.

The entire outer court, which surrounded the Holy Place and the Holy of Holies, was 150 feet by 75 feet. It was not a huge place, but it was large enough for people to come there to meet God.

In the center of the outer court was an enclosure, which was divided into two compartments. The entire enclosure measured 45 feet by 15 feet. Its height was 15 feet.

The room next to the outer court, beyond the laver, was the Holy Place. This room was 30 feet by 15 feet and was the place of fellowship. The priest entered the Holy Place through a curtain door.

The Lord Jesus Christ referred to Himself as a door, and perhaps He even had this door in mind. However, He specifically referred to the door of the sheepfold when He said, "He that entereth not by the door into the sheepfold, but climbeth up some other way, the same is a thief and a robber. But he that entereth in by the door is the shepherd of the sheep" (John 10:1,2). Jesus also referred to Himself as the door when He said, "I am the door: by me if any man enter in, he shall be saved, and shall go in and out, and find pasture" (v. 9).

No wonder Jesus said, "Come unto me, all ye that labour and are heavy laden, and I will give you rest. Take my yoke upon you, and learn of me; for I am meek and lowly in heart:

and ye shall find rest unto your souls. For my yoke is easy, and my burden is light" (Matt. 11:30).

Just beyond the Holy Place behind a veil was the Holy of Holies. Its dimensions were 15 feet by 15 feet by 15 feet. This was the place of worship in the tabernacle because the mercy seat was there. Entrance into the Holy of Holies was highly restricted, for only the high priest could enter once a year. A veil separated the Holy of Holies from the Holy Place; thus, the veil was symbolic of the entrance to God.

Jesus Christ made access to God available for all when He shed His blood on the cross. This is why Hebrews 10:19,20 says, "Having therefore, brethren, boldness to enter into the holiest by the blood of Jesus, by a new and living way, which he hath consecrated for us, through the veil, that is to say, his flesh."

### The Curtain

We will now consider the outer court in detail. When God instructed Moses concerning the tabernacle, He said, "Thou shalt make the court of the tabernacle: for the south side southward there shall be hangings for the court of fine twined linen of an hundred cubits long for one side" (Ex. 27:9). Since a cubit is about one and a half feet, one side of the tabernacle was about 150 feet long. The width of the court is stated in verse 13: "The breadth of the court on the east side eastward shall be fifty cubits [75 feet]."

The logical question that arises is, Why was this outer court necessary since God dwelt in the building proper? As we consider what God is endeavoring to teach us through the tabernacle, I think it reveals that God demands absolute separation, so there had to be a place where the priest could become separate before coming into His presence. God's presence cannot be contaminated by sin of any kind; so He was shut in from the world and the world was shut out from Him.

The wall of the outer court served as a fence that surrounded the tabernacle, opening only on the east side. Notice particularly the material used to make this curtain wall. It was made of "fine twined linen" (v. 9). The fine linen represents righteousness, as is indicated in Revelation 19:8, which says concerning the Church, "And to her was granted that she should be arrayed in fine linen, clean and white: for the fine linen is the righteousness of saints." At the Second Coming of the Lord Jesus Christ, the armies of heaven will come with Him "clothed in fine linen, white and clean" (v. 14).

So the fine linen curtain indicated that the court was encircled with the righteousness which God demands. The linen was hung on pillars and was too high for a person to climb over. No person could scale the wall of righteousness on his own; he had to enter by the gate which God had provided. The curtain wall of righteousness barred everyone, whether they were gross sinners by society's standards or whether they were self-righteous.

### The Pillars

The curtains were held up by pillars so that the fence itself was seven and a half feet in height (see Ex. 27:18). The pillars were set in a brass, or bronze, foundation which enabled them to firmly uphold the fine linen representing God's righteous standards. Brass represents judgment, and this is precisely what anyone who tried to climb over the fine linen curtain would have experienced.

There are important lessons to be learned from observing that the curtains were upheld by pillars. Sinful man was forbidden and prevented from approaching the perfect God except through the gate on the east. The wall was too high to allow any access to God without coming the prescribed way. And any who tried to climb the wall would meet certain death. The Law demanded perfect obedience.

This is why James 2:10 says, "Whosoever shall keep the whole law, and yet offend in one point, he is guilty of all." And remember, there were far more than ten laws—most Bible scholars say that there were approximately 613 commandments altogether. This shows why no one can be saved by the Law—no one could keep all 613 without offending in one point.

Luke 10 gives another illustration of the perfect obedience demanded by the Law. A lawyer came to Jesus and asked what he should do to inherit eternal life (v. 25).

Jesus asked him, "What is written in the law?" (v. 26). The lawyer answered, "Thou shalt love the Lord thy God with all thy heart, and with all thy soul, and with all thy strength, and with all thy mind; and thy neighbor as thyself" (v. 27).

Without pointing out the numerous times the individual had failed, Jesus told him, "Thou hast answered right: this do, and thou shalt live" (v. 28). The indication that the person had not lived up to the Law is seen in that he tried to justify himself. He asked, "Who is my neighbour?" (v. 29). At this point Jesus gave the parable of the Good Samaritan to teach this lawyer a valuable lesson. So we see that God's righteous standards kept out this one who wanted to justify himself by his own works.

God cannot accept man's righteousness. The Apostle Paul referred to the self-righteousness of his fellow Israelites when he wrote, "Brethren, my heart's desire and prayer to God for Israel is, that they might be saved. For I bear them record that they have a zeal of God, but not according to knowledge. For they being ignorant of God's righteousness, and going about to establish their own righteousness, have not submitted themselves unto the righteousness of God" (Rom. 10:1-3).

Those who wish to find true righteousness must find it in Christ. This is why Paul said, "For Christ is the end of the law for righteousness to every one that believeth" (v. 4). He also emphasized this point in I Corinthians 1:30: "But of him are ye in Christ Jesus, who of God is made unto us wisdom, and righteousness, and sanctification, and redemption."

Man's righteousness is despicable in the eyes of God. This is why Isaiah said, "But we are all as an unclean thing, and all our righteousnesses are as filthy rags" (Isa. 64:6).

### The Law

So the Law is not the way to God; it was never given for that purpose. Instead, it shows the sinner the righteous standards of God and bars the sinner from coming to God on his own. The Bible clearly states that no one can be saved by keeping the Law: "Therefore by the deeds of the law there shall no flesh be justified in his sight: for by the law is the knowledge of sin" (Rom. 3:20). The purpose of the Law was to make man conscious of his sin so he would see his need of coming to Christ by faith. Galatians 3:24 says, "Wherefore the law was our schoolmaster to bring us unto Christ, that we might be justified by faith."

In one respect, the wall around the tabernacle represented the Law. The Law says there is no way to come to God unless you are as good as He is. The Law was not given to save a person nor was it given to keep him saved. The Book of Galatians touches on both of these subjects. The Law was to cause man to look elsewhere for salvation rather than to himself and his own abilities. Some think they need no outside help, so it was necessary to show man how far short he was of the glory of God. This is why the Law was given. It was to reveal the terrible sinfulness of man.

Once we recognize our sinful condition and trust Jesus Christ as Saviour, we receive the indwelling Holy Spirit, who convicts of sin. Therefore, we no longer need the Law—it accomplished its purpose by showing us our need of Christ.

It is especially important to recognize that the Law does not keep us saved. We are not kept by the Law, we are "kept by the power of God through faith unto salvation ready to be revealed in the last time" (I Pet. 1:5).

All the Law could do was show a person his sinfulness, but it could not do anything about it. This is what Paul referred to when he said, "For what the law could not do, in that it was weak through the flesh, God sending his own Son in the likeness of sinful flesh, and for sin, condemned sin in the flesh: that the righteousness of the law might be fulfilled in us, who walk not after the flesh, but after the Spirit" (Rom. 8:3,4).

So although the righteousness of God excluded sinful man just as the fine linen curtain excluded man from the tabernacle, God made a way to Himself possible in the Person of Jesus Christ. Finally, the righteousness of God is placed on the account of every person who trusts Christ as Saviour. We are not naturally righteous; we become so only as we trust Jesus Christ as Saviour, for then His righteousness is placed on our account. The Bible says, "For he hath made him to be sin for us, who knew no sin; that we might be made the righteousness of God in him" (II Cor. 5:21).

## The Gate

In order for man to enter the tabernacle, he had to come through the gate. Even though the curtain of righteousness kept the people away from God, they could gain access to Him if they came in His prescribed way. This involved, first of all, entering through the gate.

Concerning the gate, God told Moses, "For the gate of the court shall be an hanging of twenty cubits, of blue, and purple, and scarlet, and fine twined linen, wrought with needlework: and their pillars shall be four, and their sockets four" (Ex. 27:16).

The gate faced east, the direction of the rising sun. There was no other entrance to the outer court, just as there is no other way to God except through Jesus Christ. Jesus said, "I am the door of the sheep. All that ever came before me are thieves and robbers: but the sheep did not hear them. I am the door: by me if any man enter in, he shall be saved, and shall go in and out, and find pasture" (John 10:7-9).

Jesus also said, "Enter ye in at the strait gate: for wide is the gate, and broad is the way, that leadeth to destruction, and many there be which go in thereat: because strait is the gate, and narrow is the way, which leadeth unto life, and few there be that find it" (Matt. 7:13,14).

As previously indicated, the gate of the tabernacle pointed to the Lord Jesus Christ, who is the only way of salvation. The New Testament abounds in references showing that Jesus Christ alone is man's only hope for salvation (see John 10:9; 14:6; Acts 4:12).

The pure linen fence, which represented the righteousness of the Lord Jesus Christ, was of one color. But the gate had four colors—blue, purple, scarlet and white (see Ex. 27:16). These colors were found throughout the tabernacle, and they, too, pointed to the Lord Jesus Christ. They symbolized several characteristics of His perfect being.

Blue is the color of heaven; it speaks of Christ's heavenly character. In this sense, the blue color represents the nature and origin of Christ.

Purple, a combination of scarlet and blue, was the color frequently associated with royalty. So this color pointed to

Jesus Christ as the king. As a mixture of blue and scarlet, purple pointed to Christ as the one who combined the heavenly nature with the sacrifice for sin. But the perfect Sacrifice was given a position of kingship over the entire universe.

Scarlet, or red, is the color of blood. This color in the gate looked ahead to Jesus Christ as the sacrifice for sin.

White symbolizes perfection; thus, it spoke of Christ's perfect character. Even when He took upon Himself a body, He "was in all points tempted like as we are, yet without sin" (Heb. 4:15).

In Philippians 2:6-11 we see the fulfillment of what the four colors in the gate of the tabernacle pointed toward. Verse 6 is a fulfillment of the blue, which speaks of heaven: "Who, being in the form of God." Fulfillment of the fine linen, or white, is also seen in this verse: "[He] thought it not robbery to be equal with God."

The scarlet, or red, is fulfilled in verse 8: "Being found in fashion as a man, he humbled himself, and became obedient unto death, even the death of the cross." The purple, or royal color, is fulfilled in verses 9-11: "Wherefore God also hath highly exalted him, and given him a name which is above every name: that at the name of Jesus every knee should bow, of things in heaven, and things in earth, and things under the earth; and that every tongue should confess that Jesus Christ is Lord, to the glory of God the Father."

These colors are seen throughout the tabernacle, except in the curtain fence, which was only white. It represented the righteousness of God and the fact that Jesus Christ perfectly fulfilled that righteousness. No wonder Paul said, "Christ is all, and in all" (Col. 3:11).

The four colors were seen on the hanging of the entrance gate, pointing to Christ, who is our entrance into eternal life. So also, the door to the Holy Place and the veil which concealed the Holy of Holies were made of the same material and colors. These all represent Christ, who is the only means of access to God. There is no other way but the Lord Jesus Christ.

## New Testament Parallels

Other parallels can also be drawn to the four colors of the tabernacle. For example, the four Gospels present Christ in a way that fulfills what the four colors pointed toward. Matthew presented Christ as the King of Israel (purple). Mark presented Christ as the suffering servant (scarlet). Luke presented Christ as the perfect man (white linen). John presented Christ as the Son of God sent from heaven (blue).

Even though there are four Gospels, there are not four ways of salvation. The four Gospel writers simply presented four different aspects of the Person of Christ, who is the one way of salvation.

The gospel itself is referred to in four different ways. The Bible speaks of the gospel of the kingdom, the gospel of the grace of God, and the everlasting gospel. Paul spoke of it as "my gospel" (Rom. 2:16). In each case, however, the basic element was the death, burial and resurrection of Jesus Christ, which provided the only way of salvation. So there was only one gospel, even though it had many different aspects.

The gate of the tabernacle was wide enough to permit access by any who desired to enter. In fact, the gate was 30 feet wide. Any who wished to enter through the gate could do so.

The Bible also emphasizes that any who wish to come to God through Christ may do so. John 3:16 says, "Whosoever believeth in him should not perish, but have everlasting life." Jesus gave an open invitation when He said, "Come unto me, all ye that labour and are heavy laden, and I will give you rest" (Matt. 11:28). The last book of the Bible gives the invitation: "The Spirit and the bride say, Come. And let him that heareth say, Come. And let him that is athirst come. And whosoever will, let him take the water of life freely" (Rev. 22:17). None is excluded; anyone who desires to come may do so.

During the time of Christ there were primarily four groups of people living in Palestine. There were the people of Israel, who gave the world God's Word. Through this nation Jesus Christ entered the world to become the Saviour of all mankind. Matthew addressed this group in his Gospel and presented Christ as the King of Israel, corresponding to the purple in the tabernacle.

The people in power during the time of Christ were the Romans. Mark wrote his Gospel to this group and presented Christ as the suffering servant, corresponding to the scarlet in the tabernacle.

The Greeks gave the world of Christ's time its culture and language. Luke addressed this group and presented Christ as the perfect man, corresponding to the linen, or white, in the tabernacle.

There was also a relatively small group of believers in Christ's time known as "Christians." To these, as well as to the world, John wrote his Gospel portraying Jesus Christ as the heaven-sent Son of God, corresponding to the blue in the tabernacle.

Although there were four classes of people during the time of Christ, anyone who wanted to come to Him for salvation was invited to do so (see Matt. 11:28; John 3:16). And Jesus promised that anyone who came to Him would not be cast out (John 6:37).

This then summarizes the message of the curtain wall and of the four-colored gate. The wall, or fence, represented God's perfect righteousness and said in effect, "Stay out." But the wide, four-colored gate spoke of the grace of God in Christ Jesus and said in effect, "Come in."

And how wonderful to realize that anyone who comes through Jesus Christ "is passed from death unto life" (John 5:24). Although there is only one door, whosoever will may come. And, as John 6:37 reveals, anyone who comes to Christ is not cast out.

Although there is only one way of salvation, Satan presents many counterfeits to mankind. However, Proverbs 14:12 warns, "There is a way which seemeth right unto a man, but the end thereof are the ways of death." Although Satan may make other ways look as attractive as the true way, we must remember that there is only one way of salvation (see John 10:1; Acts 4:12). Perhaps the one way of salvation is best summarized in the words of the Lord Jesus Christ Himself: "I am the way, the truth, and the life: no man cometh unto the Father, but by me" (John 14:6).

# Chapter 7

# The Altar and the Laver

The tabernacle did not exist throughout all of Old Testament history. It did not come into existence until after Moses led the Israelites out of Egypt. They came to Mount Sinai, and there God gave the Law and instructed Moses concerning the tabernacle.

I have thought of Job and how much he would have loved having a tabernacle in his day. When he was under severe testing, Job referred to God and said, "For he is not a man, as I am, that I should answer him, and we should come together in judgment. Neither is there any daysman betwixt us, that might lay his hand upon us both" (Job 9:32,33). Job longed for a representative to stand between himself and God, and that is precisely what the tabernacle provided at a later time.

## Purpose of the Altar

In considering the furniture in the tabernacle, we now turn our attention to the brazen altar. The altar was the place of sacrifice, and it foreshadowed the cross on which the Lord Jesus Christ shed His blood for the sins of the world.

Concerning the altar, God instructed Moses: "Thou shalt make an altar of shittim wood, five cubits long, and five cubits broad; the altar shall be foursquare: and the height thereof shall be three cubits. And thou shalt make the horns of it upon the four corners thereof: his horns shall be of the same: and thou shalt overlay it with brass" (Ex. 27:1,2).

The altar was the first piece of furniture the sinner encountered as he passed through the gate on his way to fellowship with, and the worship of, God. The altar was the meeting place for the holy God and the sinner. God came down to meet the sinner where He accepted a substitute for his sin. If man endeavored to approach God without a substitute, it meant certain death. The New Testament emphasizes, "The wages of sin is death" (Rom. 6:23). This has always been so and will always be so. The only way a person can meet God and live is to come by way of a substitute for his sin.

So the altar was actually a type of Christ, who became the substitute for man's sin and thus allowed the holy God and sinful man to meet. Even the word "altar" refers to that which is elevated or lifted up. Perhaps this is what Jesus had in mind when He said, "And I, if I be lifted up from the earth, will draw all men unto me" (John 12:32). As an offering had to be lifted up and placed on the altar, so Christ was lifted up and placed on the cross to die for the world.

The altar was the place of substitutionary sacrifices—the place of death. There the blood was poured out, and the body was consumed by fire, which speaks of judgment. The altar in the tabernacle stood between the gate of entrance and the door to fellowship with God. It barred the way so that no approach to God was possible except by the altar.

So too, the cross of Christ bars the way to God for every sinner. Those who bypass the cross will never have eternal life and fellowship with God; rather, they will remain in their condemnation.

That all must come to God by only one means is clearly evident from what Christ said to Nicodemus: "Except a man be born again, he cannot see the kingdom of God" (John 3:3). Because Nicodemus did not understand what He was saying to him, Jesus explained the necessity of spiritual birth. He said, "That which is born of the flesh is flesh; and that which is born of the Spirit is spirit" (v. 6).

The cross is the only way of salvation because it was there that Jesus shed His blood for the sin of the world. Hebrews 9:22 clearly states, "Without shedding of blood is no remission [forgiveness]." Receiving Jesus Christ as Saviour produces the only true foundation in a person's life. Paul said, "For other foundation can no man lay than that is laid, which is Jesus Christ" (I Cor. 3:11).

Sacrifices were offered daily in the Old Testament tabernacle. However, all of these sacrifices pointed forward to Jesus Christ, who would be the one sacrifice for sin forever. Concerning His one sacrifice, Hebrews 9:25-28 says, "Nor yet that he should offer himself often, as the high priest entereth into the holy place every year with blood of others; for then must he often have suffered since the foundation of the world: but now once in the end of the world hath he appeared to put away sin by the sacrifice of himself. And as it is appointed unto men once to die, but after this the judgment: so Christ was once offered to bear the sins of many; and unto them that look for him shall he appear the second time without sin unto salvation."

Hebrews 10:1 says, "For the law having a shadow of good things to come, and not the very image of the things, can never with those sacrifices which they offered year by year continually make the comers thereunto perfect." Verse 4 states, "For it is not possible that the blood of bulls and of goats should take away sins." Christ's one sacrifice forever is spoken of in verse 12: "But this man, after he had offered one sacrifice for sins for ever, sat down on the right hand of God." So Christ's one offering put away the sins that were merely covered by the Old Testament offerings and all sins since His death for those who have accepted Christ as Saviour and Lord (see Rom. 10:10).

Notice that the substitute had to be a blood sacrifice. When the Israelites were first led out of Egypt, they were delivered by a blood sacrifice. A lamb was slain, and its blood was placed on the doorposts. When God passed over the land and saw the blood, He spared the firstborn of both man and animal. Exodus 12 gives the account of this last plague which came on the Egyptians and made them willing to let the Israelites leave their land.

The Bible indicates that even as far back as the time of Cain and Abel a blood sacrifice was the only satisfactory substitute for sin in God's eyes (see Gen. 4:3-5).

Throughout the Old Testament, however, just bringing a beautiful, perfect, spotless, living lamb was not sufficient. The lamb had to be slain because atonement was only by blood. Leviticus 17:11 says, "For the life of the flesh is in the blood: and I have given it to you upon the altar to make an atonement for your souls: for it is the blood that maketh an atonement for the soul."

No matter how beautiful the lamb was and no matter how perfect its characteristics, it did not serve as a sacrifice unless it was slain. Many today extol the perfections of the Lord Jesus Christ—they admire His sinless beauty and speak of His virtues, His great teaching and His wonderful example, but none of this suffices for salvation. Without His death as a substitute (and our faith in His shed blood) there could be no transaction of salvation. We can be reconciled to God only by His death (bloodshed), not by His life.

Romans 5:8 reveals that the death of Christ was necessary: "While we were yet sinners, Christ died for us." Romans 6:23 says, "For the wages of sin is death; but the gift of God is eternal life through Jesus Christ our Lord."

Concerning His death for sin, Jesus said, "As Moses lifted up the serpent in the wilderness, even so must the Son of man be lifted up: that whosoever believeth in him should not perish, but have eternal life. For God so loved the world, that he gave his only begotten Son, that whosoever believeth in him should not perish, but have everlasting life" (John 3:14-16).

In the tabernacle, the entrance to God by way of the altar was protected by the outer court hangings upheld by poles representing the high standards of God's righteousness. However, the gate on the east, representing Christ, provided the only way into the place of sacrifice, the altar.

## Design of the Altar

The designing of the altar was not left to the guesswork of Moses. Throughout His instructions concerning the tabernacle, God emphasized accuracy in construction: "Look that thou make them after their pattern, which was shewed thee in the mount" (Ex. 25:40). Hebrews 8:5 also alludes to the tabernacle as a pattern: "Who serve unto the example and shadow of heavenly things, as Moses was admonished of God when he was about to make the tabernacle: for, See, saith he, that thou make all things according to the pattern shewed to thee in the mount."

Although the altar was made by man, it was designed by

God in heaven. So when it was completed, God was able to send the fire and ignite the wood on the altar. Man's part in the death of Christ was the making of the cross and the placing of Christ on it, just as Israel made the altar and placed the sacrifice on it. But there man's part ended because the rest involved in the death of Christ was according to the predetermined pattern and purpose of God.

Christ's death on the cross was no accident nor was God taken by surprise. It was God's plan from all eternity, as indicated by Revelation 13:8, which refers to Christ as "the Lamb slain from the foundation of the world." The first promise given to mankind concerning a Redeemer is recorded in Genesis 3:15, and the fulfillment of that promise is recorded in John 3:16. Many passages of scripture indicate that salvation through the Lord Jesus Christ was entirely according to the predestined purpose of God. God allowed mankind to make a cross and place Christ on it, but that was all He allowed man to do in the redemptive work of Christ.

In his sermon on the Day of Pentecost, Peter emphasized the part the sovereignty of God had in redemption. Peter said, "Him, being delivered by the determinate counsel and foreknowledge of God, ye have taken, and by wicked hands have crucified and slain" (Acts 2:23). So although the death of Christ was purposed beforehand, God did allow wicked men to put Christ on the cross.

The Lord Jesus Christ was a willing sacrifice for the sin of the world. "He was oppressed, and he was afflicted, yet he opened not his mouth: he is brought as a lamb to the slaughter, and as a sheep before her shearers is dumb, so he openeth not his mouth" (Isa. 53:7).

Christ was not the victim of an angry mob. He was not a martyr in a cause that had failed. By an act of His own will He laid down His life for us. Jesus said, "Therefore doth my Father love me, because I lay down my life, that I might take it again. No man taketh it from me, but I lay it down of myself. I have power to lay it down, and I have power to take it again. This commandment have I received of my Father" (John 10:17,18).

Jesus was so in control of His own life that His enemies were not able to even seize Him before His hour had come. "They sought to take him: but no man laid hands on him, because his hour was not yet come" (7:30). "No man laid hands on him; for his hour was not yet come" (8:20).

The night before His crucifixion, however, Jesus said, "The hour is come, that the Son of man should be glorified" (12:23). After making that statement, Jesus allowed Himself to be arrested, scourged and put on a cross, but no one took His life from Him. By an act of His own will, He died physically. John 19:30 says, "He said, It is finished: and he bowed his head, and gave up the ghost."

Truly, the plan of redemption reveals wonderful, infinite and unfathomable truth. We can exclaim with the Apostle Paul, "How fathomless the depths of God's resources, wisdom, and knowledge! How unsearchable His decisions, and how mysterious His methods! For who has ever understood the thoughts of the Lord, or has ever been His adviser? Or who has ever advanced God anything to have Him pay him back? For from Him everything comes, through Him everything lives, and for Him everything exists. Glory to Him forever! Amen" (Rom. 11:33-36, Williams).

### Materials in the Altar

Notice the material used in constructing the altar. It was to be made of "shittim wood" (Ex. 27:1) and was to be overlaid with "brass" (v. 2).

The wood was also known as acacia wood, which came from a tree that grew under the severe and adverse conditions of the desert. As such, it is a picture of the humanity of the Lord Jesus Christ, for He was "as a root out of a dry ground" (Isa. 53:2). In His humanity, the Lord Jesus Christ lived under the most severe conditions and gave His life in a horrible death on the cross.

Notice also that the altar was to be overlaid with brass (see Ex. 27:2). There was to be a fire on the altar day and night, so it had to have a protective surface. The word translated "brass" is more properly translated "bronze." Brass is an alloy of copper and zinc and is a product of modern technology. Bronze, however, which is a combination of copper and tin, was widely used in ancient times. However, since the King James Version uses the word "brass," this word will be used throughout this study so as not to confuse the reader.

Brass speaks of judgment, and Jesus Christ as the Son of Man was judged in the flesh for everyone's sin (see Phil. 2:6-8).

The great miracle related to the tabernacle altar made of wood was that it did not completely deteriorate and crumble under the constant heat from the fire which burned day and night. Even so, the sinless body of Christ, although in constant contact with the sin of this world, did not for one moment succumb to sin. Christ also was a constant, living miracle.

On the brazen altar were four horns, one on each corner (see Ex. 27:2). The sacrifice was bound to these horns. There was no need to bind Christ to the cross, however, for His love for us bound Him there.

Horns are also representative of power, as is evident from studying the prophecies of Daniel and Revelation. Since they were associated with salvation on the altar, they can be thought of as the power of the gospel. Paul referred to this element in the gospel when he said, "I am not ashamed of the gospel of Christ: for it is the power of God unto salvation to every one that believeth; to the Jew first, and also to the Greek" (Rom. 1:16). Paul also stated, "For the preaching of the cross is to them that perish foolishness; but unto us which are saved it is the power of God" (I Cor. 1:18).

Inasmuch as the horns pointed in all directions, they suggest that the gospel is for everyone. All were invited to approach God by bringing a sacrifice to the altar.

As you think of the gospel's extending in all directions, have you ever considered the fact that the gospel is the Good News and that "news" contains the letters of all four directions? We must not restrict the gospel to any area but must take it in every direction to a world that desperately needs to hear about Jesus Christ.

The horns on the altar also provided a place that a person could flee to and cling to if he was being persecuted or if someone was seeking his life. When Adonijah feared that Solomon would kill him, he "arose, and went, and caught hold on the horns of the altar" (I Kings 1:50). Also, after Joab, the great general, had turned against David and had cast his lot with Adonijah, in fear of his life he also "fled unto the tabernacle of the Lord, and caught hold on the horns of the altar" (2:28).

Just as the altar was a place for a person to flee to in order to obtain mercy, so the cross of Christ is the place of refuge in fleeing from the clutches of sin and Satan. At the cross the Lord Jesus Christ nullified the power of Satan. Concerning Christ, Hebrews 2:14,15 says, "Forasmuch then as the children are partakers of flesh and blood, he also himself likewise took part of the same; that through death he might destroy him that had the power of death, that is, the devil; and deliver them who through fear of death were all their lifetime subject to bondage."

Victory over Satan is found only in Jesus Christ. This is why James 4:7 says, "Submit yourselves therefore to God. Resist the devil, and he will flee from you." As we are under persecution from Satan, we need to first submit ourselves to God, and then we need to resist the Devil. Although God has allowed Satan to have freedom at this time, Satan will be cast down to the earth during the Tribulation (see Rev. 12:9). But the Tribulation saints will overcome him "by the blood of the Lamb, and by the word of their testimony" (v. 11).

### Fire on the Altar

Consider also the fire that was on the brazen altar. It was first kindled in heaven; thus, it was a divine fire. Fire often speaks of judgment in the Scriptures, and in this case the fire was never to go out. Also, there was never to be any strange, or manmade, fire made on the altar.

Only God's consuming fire of judgment was exacted on Christ as He paid the penalty of sin. Thus, the altar is a beautiful illustration of Christ, who was slain by God from the foundation of the world. No strange, or manmade, judgment was allowed to slay Christ; He gave His life of His own free will (see John 10:17,18).

This also teaches us something else concerning sin. Some people try to punish themselves for their sin, hoping to somehow be accepted by the Lord. This indicates a weak view of sin, however, for man could never punish himself sufficiently to take care of the sin issue. All judgment on sin must come from God in order for Him to be satisfied. If He judged us, we would die and be separated from Him forever in the lake of fire. But since He provided His Son to die in our place, we are delivered from the condemnation by believing in Christ as our personal Saviour.

We must realize, as Jonah did, that "salvation is of the Lord" (Jon. 2:9). The Apostle Paul also often stressed that salvation is of God. He said, "All things are of God" (II Cor. 5:18). Paul revealed that salvation is entirely of the Lord when he said, "For he hath made him to be sin for us, who knew no sin; that we might be made the righteousness of God in him" (v. 21).

God gave specific instructions that the fire on the altar should never go out. He said, "The fire upon the altar shall be burning in it; it shall not be put out: and the priest shall burn wood on it every morning, and lay the burnt-offering in order upon it, and he shall burn thereon the fat of the peace-offerings. The fire shall ever be burning upon the altar; it shall never go out" (Lev. 6:12,13).

As to the starting of the fire when the tabernacle was completed, Leviticus 9:24 says, "And there came a fire out from before the Lord, and consumed upon the altar the burnt-offering and the fat: which when all the people saw, they shouted, and fell on their faces." Thus, the fire was entirely of God, and its origin was unrelated to man. Anyone who offered manmade, or strange, fire on the altar was punished. This is precisely what happened to the sons of Aaron, Nadab and Abihu. When they offered strange fire on the altar, a fire went out from the Lord and devoured them (see Lev. 10:1-3).

This teaches us a serious lesson concerning salvation. God will not permit any mixture of human works in His plan of salvation—it is all of grace (see Eph. 2:8,9). Those who seek to be saved by their own works remain under condemnation; works can never pay the penalty for sin. Only Jesus Christ has paid the penalty; thus, the only way to be delivered from condemnation is by believing in Him as the substitute for sin.

The Scriptures make it clear that any who come to God for salvation must come in His way.

### Sacrifices on the Altar

Only God's consuming fire of judgment was exacted on Jesus Christ as He paid the penalty for sin. He was the sacrifice slain before the foundation of the world, and no strange, or madmade, efforts were allowed to mix with His sacrifice.

In Old Testament times, the consumption of the sacrifice by fire showed the people that the sacrifice had been accepted by God. Although this is not specifically mentioned in the case of Cain and Abel, that was possibly the way the Lord let them know that Abel's sacrifice was accepted and that Cain's was not (see Gen. 4:3-5).

When Elijah challenged the prophets of Baal, the sacrifice he prepared was consumed by fire from heaven. "Then the fire of the Lord fell and consumed the burnt-sacrifice, and the wood, and the stones, and the dust, and licked up the water that was in the trench" (I Kings 18:38).

When the Israelites were in the land and King Solomon built a temple designed according to the temporary tabernacle, fire again came down from heaven to consume the offering and to show God's approval. "When Solomon had made an end of praying, the fire came down from heaven, and consumed the burnt-offering and the sacrifices; and the glory of the Lord filled the house" (II Chron. 7:1).

Christ, our true sacrifice to which the Old Testament sacrifices pointed, did not need to be under God's judgment of fire throughout the ages. Because He was the God-Man, His one offering satisfied the holy demands of God forever. "We are sanctified through the offering of the body of Jesus Christ once for all" (Heb. 10:10). "This man [Jesus Christ], after he had offered one sacrifice for sins for ever, sat down on the right hand of God" (v. 12). "For by one offering he hath perfected for ever them that are sanctified" (v. 14).

Because of the effectiveness of Christ's sacrifice, God said, "Their sins and iniquities will I remember no more. Now where remission of these is, there is no more offering for sin" (vv. 17,18). The holy demands of God were satisfied once for all by the offering of Jesus Christ.

Hebrews 7:27 says of Christ: "Who needeth not daily, as those high priests, to offer up sacrifice, first for his own sins, and then for the people's: for this he did once, when he offered up himself." No wonder the Scriptures say, "Wherefore he is able also to save them to the uttermost that come unto God by him, seeing he ever liveth to make intercession for them" (v. 25).

The Old Testament priest's work was never done; he never sat down in the tabernacle. No chair was furnished for him. Hebrews contrasts the difference between an Old Testament priest and the Lord Jesus Christ: "Every priest standeth daily ministering and offering oftentimes the same sacrifices, which can never take away sins: but this man, after he had offered one sacrifice for sins for ever, sat down on the right hand of God" (10:11,12).

The Scriptures speak of Christ sitting because such an expression emphasizes His finished work of redemption. On the cross Jesus exclaimed, "It is finished" (John 19:30). This is why Hebrews 1:3 says, "When he had by himself purged our sins, sat down on the right hand of the Majesty on high." And Jesus has promised believers: "To him that overcometh will I grant to sit with me in my throne, even as I also overcame, and am sat down with my Father in his throne" (Rev. 3:21).

Because Jesus Christ has finished His work of redemption, there is a rest of faith for all who put their trust in Him. Once we have received Christ as Saviour, there is no need to return every day to the altar to reestablish the standing we have with Him. We have "everlasting life"—life that lasts forever (see John 3:16).

The spiritual rest that believers have is spoken of in Hebrews 4:9,10: "There remaineth therefore a rest to the people of God. For he that is entered into his rest, he also hath ceased from his own works, as God did from his." Christ is the end of the struggle for those who believe.

In the Old Testament tabernacle, the offerings were burnt, and the ashes were laid outside the tabernacle in a clean place. So also, after Christ offered Himself as a sacrifice for sin, His body was laid in a new tomb where no body had ever been placed.

It is possible to also think of our sins' having been reduced to ashes when Christ died for us on the cross. So when we trust Christ as Saviour, our conscience finds rest in the presence of God because sin is laid away forever. We are able to have peace when we realize that Jesus has thus dealt with our sin and that His righteous standards have been satisfied. This is not merely a feeling, but it is an actual fact. When we believe the facts of God's Word, we will have the proper feeling about these matters.

Romans 5:1 says, "Therefore being justified by faith, we have peace with God through our Lord Jesus Christ." Verses 8,9 add, "But God commendeth his love toward us, in that, while we were yet sinners, Christ died for us. Much more then, being now justified by his blood, we shall be saved from wrath through him."

Romans 8:1 assures us, "There is therefore now no condemnation to them which are in Christ Jesus." What a peace we should have from claiming the promises of verses like this! This should cause us to understand why Jesus said, "Peace I leave with you, my peace I give unto you: not as the world giveth, give I unto you. Let not your heart be troubled, neither let it be afraid" (John 14:27).

We will have peace of heart as we claim the promises of such verses as I John 1:7: "If we walk in the light, as he is in the light, we have fellowship one with another, and the blood of Jesus Christ his Son cleanseth us from all sin." The Bible tells us, "Ye were not redeemed with corruptible things, as silver and gold, from your vain conversation received by tradition from your fathers; but with the precious blood of Christ, as a lamb without blemish and without spot" (I Pet. 1:18,19).

### Construction of the Laver

The next item of tabernacle furniture beyond the brazen altar was the laver. It was in the outer court, and the priests had to stop at it for cleansing before entering the Holy Place.

God told Moses concerning the laver, "Thou shalt also make a laver of brass, and his foot also of brass, to wash withal: and thou shalt put it between the tabernacle of the congregation and the altar, and thou shalt put water therein. For Aaron and his sons shall wash their hands and their feet thereat: when they go into the tabernacle of the congregation, they shall wash with water, that they die not;

or when they come near to the altar to minister, to burn offering made by fire unto the Lord: so they shall wash their hands and their feet, that they die not: and it shall be a statute for ever to them, even to him and to his seed throughout their generations" (Ex. 30:18-21).

Exodus 38:8 reveals where Moses got the brass, or bronze, to make the laver. "He made the laver of brass, and the foot of it of brass, of the lookingglasses of the women assembling, which assembled at the door of the tabernacle of the congregation." The looking glasses, or mirrors, of that day were not made of glass but of polished bronze, and that is why Moses was able to use them in making the laver.

The order of the furniture in the tabernacle presents a beautiful picture of the progress in salvation. The brazen altar represents the cross of Christ, where faith is expressed in a substitute. This is where salvation has its starting place. This is the place where one obtains salvation through shed blood, which takes care of sin. Our justification is complete when we place our faith in Christ as our deliverer from sin. "We were reconciled to God by the death of his Son" (Rom. 5:10).

Just as the Israelites were delivered from Egypt through the shed blood of the Passover lamb, we are delivered from condemnation through the shed blood of Christ by placing faith in Him.

The second aspect of salvation has to do with separation, better known as sanctification. This aspect has to do with the believer's behavior and the need to have a cleansed life. This is so beautifully typified by the laver, which speaks of a washing by the Word. Christ said, "Now ye are clean through the word which I have spoken unto you" (John 15:3).

The third aspect of salvation has to do with the time when we will be taken from this life to be with the Lord. This is often spoken of as our glorification, for at that time we will receive changed bodies as we enter His presence (see I Cor. 15:51-53).

The laver speaks of the second aspect of salvation; that is, our separation, or sanctification. It does not relate to deliverance from condemnation—that was taken care of at the brazen altar. But having placed faith in the substitute for salvation, the believer needs to experience cleansing in his daily walk.

The New Testament reveals that every believer needs to go on to maturity. The writer of Hebrews urged, "Therefore leaving the principles of the doctrine of Christ, let us go on unto perfection [maturity]" (Heb. 6:1). There is much involved in maturity, but no believer can go on to maturity unless he stops at the laver for cleansing.

### Purpose of the Laver

Notice the purpose of the laver as it stood in the outer court of the tabernacle. The priests were to wash both their hands and their feet at the laver before proceeding into the Holy Place, the place of fellowship (see Ex. 30:21). The floor of the tabernacle was simply the dust of the desert, so the priests' feet would need daily washing. Having offered sacrifices, the priests' hands would also need to be washed.

The Bible indicates that the laver was made with an upper bowl and a lower one—one for the hands and one for the feet. This provides a beautiful parallel to the Christian life. The hands speak of service, and the feet speak of our walk. Thus, the Old Testament laver emphasizes the need to have clean hands as we serve Christ and clean feet as we walk with Him.

No priest could enter the Holy Place, not even after serving at the altar of sacrifice, until his hands and his feet were cleansed. If a priest endeavored to do so, he would die. So the laver was provided so that he would not be struck dead by God (see Ex. 30:20,21).

The Old Testament priests were types of the New Testament believers. The Bible says that Jesus Christ has "made us kings and priests unto God and his Father" (Rev. 1:6). The Apostle Peter told believers, "Ye are a chosen generation, a royal priesthood, an holy nation, a peculiar people; that ye should shew forth the praises of him who hath called you out of darkness into his marvellous light" (I Pet. 2:9).

As we consider parallels to the Old Testament priests, it is evident that we must deal with sin in our daily walk before we can expect to come into God's presence to behold His beauty, to worship Him and to fellowship with Him. A life that is not spiritually clean prevents true worship and fellowship. It does not accomplish anything to come by means of a ritualistic form of worship. This would be equivalent to bypassing the brazen altar and the laver and then expecting to experience the blessing of God in the Holy Place.

The psalmist asked, "Who shall ascend into the hill of the Lord? Or who shall stand in his holy place?" (Ps. 24:3). In the following verse, the psalmist answered his own question: "He that hath clean hands, and a pure heart" (v. 4).

We are delivered from condemnation at the altar; we are cleansed from daily defilement at the laver. The cleansing was to be repeated regularly in the tabernacle, and we also need to come regularly and daily, confessing our sins so we may have cleansing from defilement.

Whereas the brazen altar speaks of our justification, the laver speaks of our sanctification through the power of the Word. First, we need to be saved by blood. Second, we need to be free from contamination in this defiling world of sin. The power and provision for such separation is revealed in Romans 6—8. The sixth chapter lays the foundation by revealing that our separation is based on the death of Jesus Christ on the cross and that we have died with Him and have been separated from the world. Chapter 7 reveals the frustration that often comes in a believer's life as he experiences the conflict between the flesh and the Spirit. Chapter 8 reveals the victory that results when the believer walks by the Spirit.

Both aspects of salvation and separation are also seen in the experiences of Old Testament Israel. They were delivered from Egypt by blood, and later they were separated to God to walk by faith in the desert.

Today, great stress is placed on evangelism, and rightly so. But too little emphasis is given to the person's walk after he becomes a Christian. It is one thing to bring a baby into the world, but it is quite another thing to train that child as he grows to adulthood so that he will honor the Lord by the way he lives.

So often in the spiritual realm the emphasis is on birth but not on growth. I have often said that Back to the Bible is like a spiritual orphanage, ministering to those who have become Christians but have been left without proper instruction concerning how they can grow to spiritual maturity.

The aspects of salvation and growth are both seen in the Old Testament tabernacle—salvation at the altar and growth at the laver. We must always remember that the sin of the believer must be dealt with before he can enter into fellowship and really worship God. This is clearly revealed in I John 1:7-9: "But if we walk in the light, as he is in the light, we have fellowship one with another, and the blood of Jesus Christ his Son cleanseth us from all sin. If we say that we have no sin, we deceive ourselves, and the truth is not in us. If we confess our sins, he is faithful and just to forgive us our sins, and to cleanse us from all unrighteousness."

The material used for the laver was brass, or bronze. From the women's mirrors a tublike laver was made to provide a place to wash the hands and feet.

In the Bible, brass often speaks of judgment. The foundation of the poles upholding the curtain fence (representing God's righteousness) was of brass. Also, the altar, the place of sacrifice, was overlaid with brass.

### Water in the Laver

The water in the laver was symbolical of the Word of God. The Scriptures frequently speak of the cleansing that comes through the application of the Word.

The Scriptures indicate that the new birth comes through the Word. The Bible says concerning God, "Of his own will begat he us with the word of truth, that we should be a kind of firstfruits of his creatures" (James 1:18). Referring to those who have experienced the new birth, I Peter 1:23 says, "Being born again, not of corruptible seed, but of incorruptible, by the word of God, which liveth and abideth for ever."

After the new birth has taken place, the ministry of the Word is for cleansing. Jesus told believers, "Now ye are clean through the word which I have spoken unto you" (John 15:3).

The Bible reveals that the Word is specifically used in

sanctifying believers. Ephesians 5:26 indicates that Christ gave Himself for the Church "that he might sanctify and cleanse it with the washing of water by the word." In His high-priestly prayer, Jesus told the Father, "Sanctify them through thy truth: thy word is truth" (John 17:17).

At the laver then, the sins committed after regeneration by the believer are taken care of. It has to do with the defilement after the penalty of sin has been paid. The penalty was taken care of at the altar, and the cleansing is taken care of at the laver. This also indicates that cleansing comes only after regeneration, not before it.

Since the laver was made of polished brass from mirrors, the priests would easily have been able to view themselves in the brass and be sure they were entirely clean before entering the Holy Place to serve and worship.

So also, our constant contact with the world demands a daily washing by the Word. We need to read it, study it and meditate on it so it will reveal our defilement. Then we can confess our sin and be cleansed from it.

The psalmist asked, "Wherewithal shall a young man cleanse his way?" (Ps. 119:9). The same verse records the answer: "By taking heed thereto according to thy word."

How often does a person come for cleansing? No limit is mentioned. The laver contained plenty of water, so the priests could be thoroughly cleansed every time they entered the Holy Place for service and worship. Remember, their hands were symbolic of service and their feet of the Christian walk, and both needed to be cleansed from defilement.

The importance of confessing sin to the Lord is indicated in many Bible passages. We have already noted I John 1:7-9. Consider also Proverbs 28:13: "He that covereth his sins shall not prosper: but whoso confesseth and forsaketh them shall have mercy."

When Jesus was washing the disciples' feet, Peter did not want to have his feet washed. Jesus explained that if Peter would not permit it, then he would have no part with Him. This greatly concerned Peter, so he asked to be entirely washed, but Jesus said to him, "He that is washed needeth not save to wash his feet, but is clean every whit: and ye are clean, but not all" (John 13:10). At the time of salvation a person becomes spiritually clean and never needs to be saved again, but he does need to confess daily sin so he can be cleansed of its defilement.

It is important that each believer recognize what he is in Jesus Christ. First Corinthians 6:19,20 reveals that his body is a temple of the Holy Spirit. This is why Paul urged every believer to present himself to God as a living sacrifice (see Rom. 12:1,2). Whenever the believer sins, he should obey the instructions of I John 2:1,2: "If any man sin, we have an advocate with the Father, Jesus Christ the righteous: and he is the propitiation for our sins: and not for our's only, but also for the sins of the whole world."

What a wonderful God we have! He has not only provided deliverance from the penalty of sin, but He has also provided cleansing from the daily defilement of sin.

Chapter 8

# The Tabernacle Building

Whereas the outer court measured 150 feet in length and 75 feet in width, the tabernacle building itself measured only 45 feet in length, 15 feet in width and 15 feet in height.

### The Two Rooms

The first room, or compartment of the tabernacle was called the Holy Place. This room was 30 feet by 15 feet by 15 feet. It was the place of spiritual fellowship with God, and it contained three pieces of furniture. The golden candlestick symbolized Christ as the Light; the table of showbread symbolized Christ as the Bread of Life; and the altar of incense symbolized Christ as our intercessor and indicated our need to intercede for others.

The second room in the tabernacle building was known as the Holy of Holies. This room was a cube, 15 feet by 15 feet by 15 feet. It was the place of special worship, and in it was the ark of the covenant. On top of the ark was the mercy seat.

The ark of the covenant symbolized the righteous standards of God because it contained the tables of Law that God had given Moses. The standards were unattainable by man but were fulfilled in the Lord Jesus Christ.

The mercy seat on top of the ark symbolized the mercy God extends toward man on the basis of the shed blood of a substitute. Through the sacrifice of Christ, He made it possible for everyone to enter the very presence of God (see Heb. 10:19,20).

The north, south and west sides of the tabernacle

85

building were solid walls made of boards overlaid with pure gold. As such, they remind us of Christ in His humanity as well as His deity—He was the God-Man.

On the east side of the tabernacle building was a curtain, or veil, which permitted entrance to the Holy Place. The veil reminds us of Christ, who is the entrance to fellowship and worship of God.

Dividing the Holy Place from the Holy of Holies was another veil. When Jesus Christ was crucified, the veil of the temple was torn from top to bottom (see Matt. 27:51). This graphically displayed that Jesus had made access to God available to any who would come by His prescribed way. Jesus Himself was the entrance through His broken, or torn, body (see Heb. 10:19,20).

The curtains and covering of the north, south and west of the tabernacle building, as well as its top, were especially designed according to the instructions of God. The curtains and covering remind us of Christ's protection for all who are within.

### The Foundation of Silver

The tabernacle building rested on a foundation of silver. This, too, speaks of Christ, who is the foundation in every believer's life. Paul said, "For other foundation can no man lay than that is laid, which is Jesus Christ" (I Cor. 3:11).

The tabernacle building had to be placed on a solid foundation, not on the sand of the desert floor. According to Exodus 30:11-16 the silver was secured from the men 20 years of age and older. It was ransom money paid at the time of the numbering. The numbering of the men was for the purpose of war, ministry and inheritance; thus, the money was often called redemption, or atonement, money.

There is some mystery surrounding this redemption money, however, inasmuch as it could not speak of redemption from the guilt and condemnation of sin. That was by blood only. Many Scripture passages reveal that salvation is only through the blood. Leviticus 17:11 clearly says, "For it is the blood that maketh an atonement for the soul." Hebrews 9:22 says, "Without shedding of blood is no remission." And I Peter 1:18,19 says, "Forasmuch as ye know that ye were not redeemed with corruptible things, as silver and gold, from your vain conversation received by tradition from your fathers; but with the precious blood of Christ, as of a lamb without blemish and without spot."

How then can the money taken during the census be considered ransom money? The answer, I think, lies in what God told Moses in Exodus 30:12: "When thou takest the sum of the children of Israel after their number, then shall they give every man a ransom for his soul unto the Lord, when thou numberest them; that there be no plague among them, when thou numberest them." Notice especially the words "that there be no plague among them." The money was to ransom them from a plague, not from the condemnation of sin.

This ransom money, or atonement money, was to be used for the tabernacle. God told Moses, "Thou shalt take the atonement money of the children of Israel, and shalt appoint it for the service of the tabernacle of the congregation; that it may be a memorial unto the children of Israel before the Lord, to make an atonement for your souls" (v. 16).

Whenever a census was taken, there was always the danger of pride. A numbering of the people would reveal their military strength, and the tendency would be to trust in numbers rather than in God. Second Samuel 24 and I Chronicles 21 reveal that David sinned in numbering the people. The Bible indicates that he depended on the strength of his people rather than on God's ability to deliver him from the enemy. Because of David's sin a plague came on Israel and 70,000 died from it.

Gideon was an example of one who learned to trust God rather than rely on any specific number of men (see Judges 7:1-6). Gideon began with an army of 32,000. But the Lord kept having him send men away until he was left with only 300 men. Then the Lord gave victory to Gideon and his army because they were forced to trust in Him rather than in their own strength.

All this provides background to understanding why God caused a ransom to be paid at the time Israel was numbered. It served as a constant reminder to the men not to trust in their own strength. Money had to be given in order to keep a plague from coming on them because of their pride. It was

God's way of reminding them that they were merely ransomed (redeemed) men and that without this redemption they were nothing.

This should serve as a reminder to us today that we are not to depend on our own strength. Having received Christ as Saviour, we are a redeemed people, for we have been bought with a price (see I Cor. 6:20).

Those in Israel's army were really in the army of God because they were redeemed for that purpose. We, too, are not to be serving ourselves but the Lord because we owe everything to Him.

The ransom money was also called "atonement money" (see Ex. 30:16). The word "atonement" means "to cover." It does not mean "at-one-ment" since only Christ can make us one with God.

Money was given at the census because of potential pride in numbers, and it covered the sin even before it was committed. This ransom money was later collected and used in the service of the tabernacle. It was not a freewill offering; it was a requirement.

Since the tabernacle stood on the silver foundation, it pointed to our redemption in Christ. We are redeemed from an evil world of corruption and are set aside to the sacred service of the Lord.

In ourselves we are nothing, but based on the redemptive work of Christ, we are empowered and enriched by Him. This is emphasized in what Jesus said: "Abide in me, and I in you. As the branch cannot bear fruit of itself, except it abide in the vine; no more can ye, except ye abide in me" (John 15:4). The Apostle Paul made Jesus Christ the focal point of his life. This is why he told the Corinthians, "I determined not to know any thing among you, save Jesus Christ, and him crucified" (I Cor. 2:2).

Having trusted Jesus Christ as Saviour, "we are his workmanship, created in Christ Jesus unto good works, which God hath before ordained that we should walk in them" (Eph. 2:10).

Our standing with God—concerning both redemption and service—is only because of what we are in Christ Jesus. It is never based on our own attainment.

## The Boards

The boards of the Old Testament tabernacle also have rich significance for us today. God told Moses, "Thou shalt make boards for the tabernacle of shittim wood standing up" (Ex. 26:15).

The acacia, or shittim, wood was from a tree that grew in the dry, barren desert. As such, it was a fitting symbol of the humanity of Christ, for He was spoken of "as a root out of a dry ground" (Isa. 53:2). This wood was covered with gold, which typified the deity and glory of Christ. So two aspects of Christ were revealed in the boards: The acacia wood indicated Christ's humanity, and the gold overlay indicated His deity. Jesus Christ was with the Father from all eternity past, but He "was made flesh, and dwelt among us" (John 1:14).

The boards are also a picture of the individual believer's standing in Christ. Each person who trusts Christ as Saviour stands complete in Him. The boards of the tabernacle building stood upright on a solid base of silver and were connected with rods (see chart). Just as the boards were united in the tabernacle building, so the believer is united to Christ.

The night before His crucifixion, Christ specifically prayed concerning our being united to Him (see John 17:21-23). Ephesians 1:4-6 also tells of the relationship we have with Christ. How thankful we can be for the statement in verse 6: "Wherein he hath made us accepted in the beloved."

The boards of the tabernacle rested on a foundation of silver. This is a beautiful picture of the believer, who is in the world and yet not of it. Galatians 1:4 tells of Christ "who gave himself for our sins, that he might deliver us from this present evil world, according to the will of God and our Father." Although we live in the world, Christ has delivered us from the evil world system.

Each board may also represent the individual believer in that once the board was part of the desert tree and became a part of the tabernacle of God. But a process was needed to get it from the tree to the tabernacle. The ax had to be applied, and then there was a drying process. Eventually the board was stripped of its natural beauty and covered with gold, representative of God's nature. Like the boards of the tabernacle, God has taken us from the world and has given us a new nature. We are united to Him and are fitted into the Body precisely as He has chosen (see I Cor. 12).

Exodus 26:26-28 reveals that the boards were held together by bars made of acacia wood. These, too, were overlaid with gold, so they also typified the deity of the Lord Jesus Christ. Notice especially that "the middle bar in the midst of the boards shall reach from end to end" (v. 28). All the boards were united into one.

What a beautiful picture this is of individual believers who are united in the Body of Christ. The New Testament tells us, "For as the body is one, and hath many members, and all the members of that one body, being many, are one body: so also is Christ. For by one Spirit are we all baptized into one body, whether we be Jews or Gentiles, whether we be bond or free; and have been all made to drink into one Spirit. For the body is not one member, but many" (I Cor. 12:12-14).

The Book of Ephesians uses the analogy of a building in showing how believers fit together: "In whom all the building fitly framed together groweth unto an holy temple in the Lord: in whom ye also are builded together for an habitation of God through the Spirit" (2:21,22).

### The Covering of Badgers' Skins

Because of the sandstorms and occasional rain that could occur in the desert, it was necessary for the tabernacle to be properly covered. God gave Moses specific instructions about the coverings. These instructions are recorded in Exodus 26:1-14.

There were four coverings, and they typified Christ as the protection both to God's perfect holiness and to man's perfect standing in Christ.

The outer covering was referred to as "a covering above of badgers' skins" (v. 14). This was the outer covering; it was on top of the others.

These were not badgers as we know them in the western world; such animals were not found in the Middle East.

Rather, the animal was a porpoise—a marine animal plentiful in the Nile region. The porpoise skin was very durable and was used for such things as shoes. Thus, it provided perfect protection against the elements of the desert.

Only this outer covering was visible to the public. There was nothing beautiful about it. It was bleached by the sun and wind of the desert. This outer covering gave no indication of the beauty of the interior of the tabernacle.

As such, the outer covering was a perfect picture of the humanity of the Lord Jesus Christ. As viewed by the unbeliever, there was nothing attractive in Jesus Christ. Isaiah prophesied of Him, "He hath no form nor comeliness; and when we shall see him, there is no beauty that we should desire him. He is despised and rejected of men" (Isa. 53:2,3).

Just as a person had to come to the inside of the tabernacle to see its beauty, a person needs to receive Jesus Christ as Saviour and thus enter into fellowship with Him in order to fully appreciate the beauty of His holiness.

Now that Jesus has ascended to the Heavenly Father after finishing His work of redemption, He has chosen to reveal Himself through believers. The only way for the world to see Him now is to see Him in us. Jesus revealed the Father to believers so they in turn may be able to reveal Him to the world (see John 17:6).

Inasmuch as unbelievers fail to appreciate the beauty of Christ, it is understandable if they fail to appreciate our testimony for Him. However, we should live consistent, upright lives so others will desire to know our Lord and Master.

In prophesying the rejection that Jesus would experience from the world that could not see His beauty, Psalm 22:6,7 says, "But I am a worm, and no man; a reproach of men, and despised of the people. All they that see me laugh me to scorn: they shoot out the lip, they shake the head." Isaiah prophesied concerning Christ, "As many were astonied at thee; his visage was so marred more than any man, and his form more than the sons of men" (Isa. 52:14).

So today the world sees no beauty in Jesus Christ; He is blasphemed, and His name is used in vain. But praise God there are those who recognize their sinful condition and realize that their only hope is to trust in Christ as personal

Saviour. These who come to the "inside" are those who truly behold His beauty.

The outer covering provided a protection to all within the tabernacle. Thus, it was typical of Christ, who is our protection.

The exposed portion is a fitting picture of the Lord's body as He bore our sins. They placed a crown of thorns on His head, spit on Him, struck Him and scourged Him. They pierced His side when He was hanging on the cross, and they exposed Him to humiliating shame. All of this caused the onlookers to be further convinced of His unattractiveness, which in itself was a fulfillment of Old Testament prophecies.

### The Covering of Rams' Skins

The second cover, the one under the top covering, was of "rams' skins dyed red" (Ex. 26:14). This covering was not visible to the public, yet it was needed for the further protection of the tabernacle. Since there were four coverings in all, this covering could not be seen from the outside or the inside.

The ram was an animal used for a substitutionary sacrifice. Such a sacrifice took the place of a person destined to die because of his sin.

In the New Testament, Mark's Gospel presents Christ as the suffering substitute. Man was under condemnation, but Jesus Christ died in his place so that any who receive Christ as Saviour are delivered from condemnation.

For the covering, the rams' skins were tanned and dyed a deep crimson. The skins were joined together in such a way that they provided a complete covering of protection for all that was underneath it.

The red skins spoke of sacrifice and pointed to Jesus Christ, who is the sacrifice for sin. The first mention in the Bible of skins for a covering is Genesis 3:21. Because Adam had sinned and had broken his relationship with God, he noticed that he and Eve were naked. Their sin had exposed them to shame. Although they tried to cover their shame with aprons made of fig leaves, they were unable to cover their sin by their own efforts.

After confronting them with their sin, God provided a

covering for them. He could not accept their manmade coverings, so He provided coverings made from the skins of animals. "Unto Adam also and to his wife did the Lord God make coats of skins, and clothed them" (Gen. 3:21). The covering God provided was an evidence of His grace and love. God would have been completely righteous in showing no mercy at all, but instead He provided a covering.

In order for a covering of skins to be made for Adam and Eve, there had to be a substitute. An animal had to die so the coverings could be made. This became the standard for all substitutionary sacrifices thereafter; there was to be no deviation. A sacrificial animal had to be brought before God as a substitute for the individual's sin.

Cain tried to deviate from this requirement, but God would not accept his offering of the fruit of the ground (see 4:3-5). Abel, on the other hand, brought "of the firstlings of his flock" (v. 4), and God accepted his offering because it was a blood sacrifice.

A key incident in Abraham's life revealed the significance of the ram as a substitutionary sacrifice. God asked Abraham to sacrifice his son, and as Abraham was in the process of doing so the Lord said, "Lay not thine hand upon the lad, neither do thou any thing unto him: for now I know that thou fearest God, seeing that thou hast not withheld thy son, thine only son from me" (22:12). Then notice the significant statement that follows: "And Abraham lifted up his eyes, and looked, and behold behind him a ram caught in a thicket by his horns: and Abraham went and took the ram, and offered him up for a burnt-offering in the stead of his son" (v. 13).

Earlier, when Isaac had asked, "Where is the lamb for a burnt-offering?" (v. 7), Abraham had said, "God will provide himself a lamb for a burnt-offering" (v. 8). At that time Abraham did not know how, but later he saw it with his own eyes.

Abraham was full of praise to God, and he called the place "Jehovah-jireh" (v. 14), meaning "the Lord will provide." In this case, the Lord provided a substitute for Isaac.

This incident took place on Mount Moriah where the temple was later located. In the same general area Christ was crucified on Calvary. Therefore, the ram was a significant picture of Jesus Christ, who was the substitute for sinners.

This covering of rams' skins dyed red on the tabernacle provided a safe and protected place for the priest to minister in behalf of the people who had offered a sacrifice. Only as we are in Christ are we truly protected.

### The Covering of Goats' Hair

The covering underneath the rams' skin was made of goats' hair (see Ex. 26:7). In the Bible, a goat is frequently used as a symbol of sin. This covering was immediately on top of the beautiful linen covering that could be seen from within the tabernacle.

The covering made of goats' hair represents Christ as the sin offering. It is significant to understand how Christ was represented in each of the coverings. The outer covering of badgers', or porpoises', skins represented Christ as the despised One. The second covering of rams' skins represented Christ as the substitute through death. The third covering of goats' hair represented Christ as the sin offering. And the fourth, or inner, covering represented the beauty of Christ's perfect life seen in all of His positional functions as king, servant, perfect man and perfect God. Later, the inner covering will be discussed in detail.

In considering the third covering of goats' hair, we are reminded that Christ is our sin-bearer, even as two goats were used on the Day of Atonement to reveal this.

Leviticus 16 tells of the use of two goats on the Day of Atonement. One goat was slain at the altar, and his blood was poured out there (v. 15). This goat symbolized the sacrifice of Jesus Christ. Then the priest placed his hands on the living goat and confessed over it the sins of Israel. He then sent it into the wilderness, never to return. This goat symbolized the fact that Jesus Christ has removed our sins as far as the east is from the west. When a person trusts Christ as his Saviour, the penalty of his sins is paid forever, and he is delivered from all condemnation.

We must never forget that Jesus Christ is the One who has borne all our sin. "All we like sheep have gone astray; we have turned every one to his own way; and the Lord hath laid on him the iniquity of us all" (Isa. 53:6). Although some teach that even Satan has a part in bearing the sin of mankind, there is no scriptural support for this view. Satan will bear his own sin and will someday be cast into the lake of fire to be tormented forever, but he in no way bears the sin of others (see Rev. 20:10).

The sin of mankind was placed on Jesus Christ when He was upon the cross; thus, II Corinthians 5:21 says, "He hath made him to be sin for us, who knew no sin; that we might be made the righteousness of God in him."

In the Garden of Gethsemane, Jesus prayed, "Father, if thou be willing, remove this cup from me: nevertheless not my will, but thine, be done" (Luke 22:42). What cup was Jesus referring to? Since He feared nothing but sin, it is likely that Christ was referring to the cup of sin, not death itself. Christ willingly laid down His life for us, as John 10:17,18 indicates: "I lay down my life, that I might take it again. No man taketh it from me, but I lay it down of myself. I have power to lay it down, and I have power to take it again."

In His purity, the Lord Jesus Christ shrank from sin. He saw this cup and prayed three times that it might be removed from Him. But He did not pray that death be removed from Him. Jesus knew that He would be spiritually separated from the Father when He hung on the cross with our sins upon Him. Because He had all the sin of mankind upon Him, Christ was forsaken by God, and this is why He called out from the cross, "My God, my God, why hast thou forsaken me?" (Matt. 27:46). Because He is holy and cannot look on sin, God had to turn His back on His only begotten Son while He died on the cross in our place. But in His mercy, God brought darkness on the world so people could not view Christ's awful agony during these hours.

On the cross, Christ paid the price for sin, just as the slain goat did on the Day of Atonement. And as the live goat, He carried away forever the sin of those who have trusted Him as Saviour.

When Christ's work of redemption was finished on the cross, light again broke upon the world, and the veil of the temple was torn in two (see Heb. 10:19,20). Access into the very presence of God had been made available to all who would come the prescribed way. Although God Himself had made salvation possible, only those who personally accept, or appropriate, Christ as their substitute will be delivered from their sins. Those who refuse to accept Him as their substitute remain in their sins and under a state of condemnation (see John 3:18).

Confession and repentance are absolutely necessary, as well as personally appropriating what Christ has done for us. Proverbs 28:13 says, "He that covereth his sins shall not prosper: but whoso confesseth and forsaketh them shall have mercy." Jesus said, "Except ye repent, ye shall all likewise perish" (Luke 13:3).

### The Covering of Linen

The fourth, or inner, covering of the tabernacle was made of "fine twined linen" (Ex. 26:1). As this passage indicates, there were to be various colors woven into it—blue, purple and scarlet.

When the tabernacle was erected, this was the first covering placed over the tabernacle building, and then the other coverings were placed on top. This covering was the only one seen from within the tabernacle. Although the exterior covering was unattractive, this interior covering was beautiful, emphasizing again that only when we are on the inside with Christ can we realize His true beauty.

The fine linen was embroidered with figures of cherubim in blue, purple and scarlet. Thus, this linen represented Christ in all of His glory and perfect righteousness. The white linen represents the sinless, righteous Christ. Blue, the heavenly color, represents His heavenly origin or nature. Scarlet represents His sacrificial death. Purple—a combination of blue and scarlet—represents His royal character; that is, His kingly and sovereign nature and stately splendor.

The design of cherubim with outstretched wings were woven into the linen. Thus, they hovered over the priests who were ministering to the Lord in the tabernacle.

In the Bible, cherubim are seen as guardians of the holiness of God. Here, the cherubim represented protection given to those in the tabernacle. Cherubim are first mentioned in Genesis 3:24. They appeared on the east side of the Garden of Eden to guard "the way of the tree of life." In this sense, they guarded the holiness of God in His mercy for man.

As the priests ministered in the tabernacle and looked upward, they saw the cherubim and were reminded that God was watching and protecting them. The psalmist recognized that the Lord watches over His own. He wrote: "Behold, the eye of the Lord is upon them that fear him, upon them that hope in his mercy; to deliver their souls from death, and to keep them alive in famine" (Ps. 33:18,19).

The world on the outside saw none of this beauty or the symbolism of the protecting hand of God. This is another reminder that the natural man does not understand the things of God because he is spiritually blind (see I Cor. 2:14; II Cor. 4:3,4). Only those who have been born again can spiritually see the glories of God. After Paul believed in Christ on the road to Damascus, his greatest desire was to know more of the glory of Christ. He counted everything in the past as worthless in comparison to knowing Jesus Christ as Saviour and being found in Him without blame (see Phil. 3:7-9). Paul's desire to know more about the Lord is clearly expressed in Philippians 3:10: "That I may know him, and the power of his resurrection, and the fellowship of his sufferings, being made conformable unto his death."

We will be different individuals when we truly see the glory of God. When Job saw God's glory, he said, "I have heard of thee by the hearing of the ear: but now mine eyes seeth thee. Wherefore I abhor myself, and repent in dust and ashes" (Job 42:5,6).

Just to be satisfied with salvation (to stop at the brazen altar) is lamentable. The more time we spend on the inside of the sanctuary at the table of showbread, the altar of incense and the golden candlestick, the more we will behold and appreciate His beauty.

Chapter 9
# The Door to the Holy Place

As one entered the tabernacle's outer court from the east, he first came to the brazen altar and then to the laver. Having made proper sacrifice at the altar and having been cleansed at the laver, the priest was then prepared to enter the Holy Place.

A curtain served as a door to the Holy Place. God instructed Moses, "Thou shalt make an hanging for the door of the tent [the Holy Place], of blue, and purple, and scarlet, and fine twined linen, wrought with needlework. And thou shalt make for the hanging five pillars of shittim wood, and overlay them with gold, and their hooks shall be of gold: and thou shalt cast five sockets of brass for them" (Ex. 26:36,37).

## Contrasts Between the Door and the Veil

Many contrasts can be drawn between the door of the Holy Place and the veil of the Holy of Holies. Even though both were curtains, we will refer to the entrance of the Holy Place as a "door" and to the entrance of the Holy of Holies as the "veil" to distinguish the two.

The door gave the priest entrance from the outer court after he had come by way of the gate, altar and laver, where a proper relationship was established. The door of the Holy Place provided access to fellowship with God.

On the other hand, the veil gave the priest entrance from the Holy Place, a place of fellowship, to the Holy of Holies, a place of worship.

The door to the Holy Place did not have cherubim

embroidered on it, whereas the veil to the Holy of Holies did. The cherubim speak of protection, as we noted concerning the covering viewed from within the temple.

The door of the Holy Place was designed for entrance, whereas the veil of the Holy of Holies was designed to keep people out.

The door had five pillars, set on a foundation of brass, holding the curtains. The veil had four pillars, set in a foundation of silver, holding the curtains.

In all of these contrasts, one outstanding difference between the door of the Holy Place and the veil of the Holy of Holies seems to stand out. The door was to give entrance to the priests as they daily ministered, whereas the veil shut out everyone from the presence of God except the high priest, who was permitted to enter once a year with the blood of the atonement goat. The hangings of the door to the Holy Place were designed in such a way that frequent access was possible.

The door to the Holy Place was located on the east end of the tabernacle building. This reminds us of the cherubim who were placed on the east of the Garden of Eden after Adam and Eve had fallen into sin. The cherubim were placed there to guard the way of the tree of life (see Gen. 3:24).

Adam and Eve were banished from the Garden of Eden because of sin, but in the tabernacle we see God's move to bring man back to Himself. The tabernacle, with its altar, provided a place of sacrifice so man could once again find the entrance to the door into the place of fellowship with God. But man was barred from the Holy of Holies, the immediate presence of God, until the death of Jesus Christ when the veil was torn in two and access was made available (see Matt. 27:51; Heb. 10:19,20).

## Material in the Door

Notice the material that was to be used for the door to the Holy Place. God told Moses, "Thou shalt make an hanging for the door of the tent, of blue, and purple, and scarlet, and fine twined linen, wrought with needlework" (Ex. 26:36). This fine linen with three colors of needlework was similar to the gate of the outer court, which permitted entrance to the entire tabernacle area. This serves as another reminder that there is only one entrance through which any person can come into fellowship with God. That entrance is through Jesus Christ, the eternal, incarnate Son of God who died for the sin of mankind, rose again, and ascended to the right hand of the Father.

In the door to the Holy Place were the colors that pointed to the Lord Jesus Christ. Blue pointed to His heavenly nature, scarlet to His sacrifice, and purple to His kingly nature. This door was supported by high pillars of acacia wood overlaid with gold, pointing to the God-Man nature of Christ (see v. 37).

Although the hangings of the door shut off the Holy Place from the outer court, it formed an entrance for those who were qualified. In the case of tabernacle worship, only the priests were qualified to enter. Now, however, we do not come to a tabernacle to worship. Every believer is qualified to enter the presence of God because all believers comprise "a royal priesthood" (I Pet. 2:9).

There were no cherubim on the door to the Holy Place. The cherubim protected the holiness of God, but the door represented Jesus Christ Himself. Jesus said, "I am the door" (John 10:7-9). Although He was using the analogy of the shepherd and the sheep on this occasion, Jesus said, "I am the door: by me if any man enter in, he shall be saved, and shall go in and out, and find pasture" (v. 9). And Christ assured us concerning the shepherd, "When he putteth forth his own sheep, he goeth before them, and the sheep follow him: for they know his voice" (v. 4). Jesus stated the purpose of His coming when He said, "I am come that they might have life, and that they might have it more abundantly" (v. 10). These verses reveal three privileges for believers: to go in and out, for He is the doorway to fellowship; to follow the Shepherd, who always goes before us; to have abundant life as well as eternal life.

### Pillars of the Door

Concerning the door to the Holy Place, God told Moses, "Thou shalt make for the hanging five pillars of shittim wood, and overlay them with gold, and their hooks shall be of gold: and thou shalt cast five sockets of brass for them" (Ex. 26:37).

As indicated previously, the acacia wood speaks of the humanity of Christ, and the gold speaks of His deity. The combination of the two represents Jesus Christ as the God-Man. As such, He upholds the curtain which allows entrance to the Holy Place. Not only is He the curtain, or the door, to fellowship, but He even upholds it Himself as He invites every qualified person to enter for priestly privileges.

The special privileges of believers are not set forth in the Old Testament or in the Gospels; they are revealed in the New Testament Epistles. There were five writers of the Epistles—Paul, Peter, James, John and Jude. Paul referred to Peter, James and John as "pillars" (Gal. 2:9). All five of these men were pillars of the Church in that they upheld Christ's teachings concerning what was necessary for fellowship with Him.

The door to the Holy Place was set in foundations of brass (see Ex. 26:37). Brass speaks of judgment, in this case, the judgment on Christ for sin. These pillars pointed toward the complete judgment on Christ, and thus they upheld the inviting curtains of entrance made possible by the finished work of Calvary. So they reminded the worshiper that Christ is the door because of His suffering and death on behalf of mankind. Jesus alluded to the purpose of the curtain when He said, "I am the way, the truth, and the life: no man cometh unto the Father, but by me" (John 14:6).

# Chapter 10

# The Table of Showbread

On entering the Holy Place, the priest would see an item of furniture on his right commonly known as the table of showbread. This highly significant piece of furniture pointed to the Lord Jesus Christ. Before we consider the table of showbread in more detail, however, it would be well to briefly consider the other items of furniture in the tabernacle.

## Seven Pieces of Furniture

The tabernacle contained seven pieces of furniture in all. Seven is the number of perfection in the Bible, so the seven pieces of furniture speak to us of God's perfect provision for those who are in Christ.

Follow the seven steps as a person on the outside (where a sinner may behold Christ merely as a man) enters and grows in the knowledge of Christ.

We have already considered the altar and the laver in detail. Remember, the altar was a picture of the cross of Christ, for it was there that He purchased our redemption through the shedding of His blood. "Without shedding of blood is no remission" (Heb. 9:22).

The laver, which was in the outer court next to the tabernacle building, was for the washing of the priest's hands and feet. Thus, it speaks of separation from the world and cleansing from defilement. The laver reminds us of the Bible, the Word of God, because we are "clean through the word" (John 15:3).

Then stepping inside of the Holy Place, the priest was in

the place of fellowship. On the right was the table of showbread, straight ahead was the altar of incense, and to his left was the golden candlestick. The table of showbread speaks of Christ, who is the Bread of Life; the altar of incense speaks of our worship and prayers ascending to God; the golden lampstand speaks of Christ as the Light of the World and reminds us of the Holy Spirit, who illumines our way.

Beyond the Holy Place through the veil was the Holy of Holies, the place of worship. The last two pieces of furniture—the ark of the covenant and the mercy seat—were in this room. The ark of the covenant represented God's final authority and our need to be fully surrendered to Him. On top of the ark was the mercy seat made of pure gold, which speaks of the fact that our only hope is in the mercy of God, made possible by the shed blood that provides access to God.

All seven pieces of furniture pointed toward the Lord Jesus Christ, who completely satisfied the holiest demands of God concerning sin. As sinners, we are delivered from condemnation, and we receive eternal life only by believing in Jesus Christ as our substitute for sin.

Notice that the Holy Place contained three pieces of furniture—the table of showbread, the golden lampstand and the altar of incense.

Although each was a distinct piece of furniture, each one related to the other. It is impossible to understand the full significance of one without understanding the others.

The table of showbread speaks of Christ, the Living Word on whom we are to feed to receive spiritual nourishment. The golden lampstand on the other side of the Holy Place cast light on the table of showbread. In this sense, the pieces of furniture related to each other.

So also, as we study the Word of God and are enabled by the Holy Spirit to understand it, we will grow in our knowledge and appreciation of Jesus Christ, the Bread of Life.

The lampstand provided the only light within the tabernacle building. Only the light which God specified was allowed in the building. This is a reminder to us that the world's knowledge cannot throw light on the Word of God or on the Person of Christ. Only the Holy Spirit can illuminate truths concerning the Word and the Person of Christ.

In the Holy Place, standing next to the veil leading to the Holy of Holies, was the altar of incense. This was the place of expression to God by way of intercession. As we study the Word of God, which is illuminated to us by the Holy Spirit, we come to the place of intercessory prayer.

Notice who was allowed into the Holy Place and what its purpose was. Only the priests could enter the Holy Place of the tabernacle; only they had been set aside for spiritual ministry to the Lord in behalf of the people. However, today all believers are considered "a royal priesthood" (I Pet. 2:9), so every believer is allowed to enter the presence of God. All of us who have trusted Christ as Saviour have the opportunity and privilege of entering the Holy Place to fellowship with God by feeding on the Word, which is illumined to us by the Holy Spirit. Then we can spend time at the altar of intercession.

Our relationship with God is established in the outer court at the altar of sacrifice and at the laver of cleansing. In the Holy Place, our fellowship is established and maintained by the study of the Word, by the illuminating work of the Holy Spirit, and by the prayer of intercession. Because all of these elements point to Christ, it is no wonder that Jesus said what He did as recorded in John 15: "Now ye are clean through the word which I have spoken unto you" (v. 3). This parallels the purpose of the laver in the tabernacle.

Jesus also said, "Abide in me, and I in you. As the branch cannot bear fruit of itself, except it abide in the vine; no more can ye, except ye abide in me. I am the vine, ye are the branches: he that abideth in me, and I in him, the same bringeth forth much fruit: for without me ye can do nothing" (vv. 4,5). This parallels the table of showbread and the golden lampstand in the tabernacle. We are to learn of Christ and to realize that we can do nothing without Him. He is revealed to us through the Word as the Holy Spirit illuminates it to our minds. And Jesus promised, "If ye abide in me, and my words abide in you, ye shall ask what ye will, and it shall be done unto you" (v. 7). This parallels the altar of incense. Every believer is to spend time in prayer, bringing the needs of others and his own needs before God.

## The Table

Notice the instructions God gave Moses concerning the table of showbread: "Thou shalt also make a table of shittim wood: two cubits shall be the length thereof, and a cubit the breadth thereof, and a cubit and a half the height thereof. And thou shalt overlay it with pure gold, and make thereto a crown of gold round about" (Ex. 25:23,24).

As indicated previously, the acacia wood speaks of the humanity of Christ. However, it was overlaid with pure gold, which speaks of the deity of Christ. The combination of the two reminds us that Jesus Christ was the God-Man. Although Christ took upon Himself human flesh, He was also God; therefore, He did not have a sin nature as other men do. As the Bible says, "In him is no sin" (I John 3:5).

On the table which God instructed Moses to build, God said, "And thou shalt set upon the table shewbread before me alway" (Ex. 25:30).

The bread on the table was a beautiful symbol of Christ's body. The bread was made from the fine flour which resulted from a grinding process. This speaks of Christ, who experienced extreme suffering yet retained His sinless purity.

The bread was baked, which meant it was exposed to heat. This reminds us of the heat of torment that Jesus Christ experienced when Israel rejected Him as Messiah and crucified Him for claiming to be the Son of God.

The bread was also to be unleavened. Leaven is used in the Bible as a symbol of sin. Since the bread was unleavened, it was a beautiful symbol of the sinless Christ.

The bread was the result of a process of death and suffering, for the wheat had been harvested, ground to powder and baked in a hot oven. So also, Christ went through the crushing experience of Gethsemane and the burning heat of Calvary.

We need to keep in mind all that Jesus Christ went through to procure our salvation. As we read the Scriptures and realize that He sweat, as it were, drops of blood and then writhed in agony on the cross, we will be repulsed by empty religions that offer only a mere formality of worship. When we realize what Jesus Christ went through for us, we will heed the Scriptures and present ourselves to Him completely for worship and service. Romans 12:1,2 tells all believers, "Present your bodies a living sacrifice, holy, acceptable unto God, which is your reasonable service. And be not conformed to this world: but be ye transformed by the renewing of your mind, that ye may prove what is that good, and acceptable, and perfect, will of God."

## God's Provision

The tabernacle was God's provision for Israel during the wilderness journey, and the provision was seen especially in the table of showbread, symbolizing spiritual food. The Israelites had been delivered from judgment on the firstborn by the blood of the lamb, and they had been separated from Egypt by the power of God at the Red Sea.

Egypt is sometimes used in the Scriptures as a symbol of the world. Although the Israelites were still in the world, they were not of the world; that is, they were not part of Egypt any longer. They were on the march through the barren desert, and only the power of God could sustain them there. The desert was not meant to be their permanent dwelling place; they were only marching through it on the way to Canaan.

The nation of Israel is a picture of the individual believer who, during his earthly life, passes through the world even though he is not a part of it. The Bible says of Abraham, "By faith he sojourned in the land of promise, as in a strange country, dwelling in tabernacles [tents] with Isaac and Jacob, the heirs with him of the same promise: for he looked for a city which hath foundations, whose builder and maker is God" (Heb. 11:9,10). Those in the Old Testament looked ahead by faith to the provision God would someday make for sin. God accepted their blood sacrifices, given in faith, as a covering for their sin until Christ would take it away. But, verse 13 says, "These all died in faith, not having received the promises, but having seen them afar off, and were persuaded of them, and embraced them, and confessed that they were strangers and pilgrims on the earth."

Each of us who knows Christ as Saviour needs to ask, What is my attitude toward the world? What our attitude should be is stated in Titus 2:11-13: "For the grace of God that bringeth salvation hath appeared to all men, teaching us that, denying ungodliness and worldly lusts, we should live soberly, righteously, and godly, in this present world; looking for that blessed hope, and the glorious appearing of the great God and our Saviour Jesus Christ."

Galatians 1:4 tells what Jesus Christ has done for us: "Who gave himself for our sins, that he might deliver us from this present evil world, according to the will of God and our Father." Jesus came to deliver us not only from the guilt of sin but also from the power of sin—"from this present evil world."

Because we are not of the world even though we are in it, we should not expect the world to love us. Jesus told His disciples, "If ye were of the world, the world would love his own: but because ye are not of the world, but I have chosen you out of the world, therefore the world hateth you" (John 15:19).

Even though we might experience much difficulty in this world, let us remember the words of Christ: "These things I have spoken unto you, that in me ye might have peace. In the world ye shall have tribulation: but be of good cheer; I have overcome the world" (16:33).

The table of showbread in the tabernacle was to be a constant reminder to the Israelites that God was their provision for the wilderness journey. Because it was symbolic of spiritual food, it pointed to Jesus Christ, who came to die that all who receive Him as Saviour might also have abundant life (see 10:10). Jesus has given us the Word, and we are to feed on it. It is there that we learn of Him and gain spiritual sustenance and growth.

The psalmist emphasized the importance of God's Word. In the longest chapter in the Bible, Psalm 119, the psalmist frequently referred to the place of the Word of God in the believer's life. Notice several verses from this great psalm.

"Wherewithal shall a young man cleanse his way? By taking heed thereto according to thy word" (v. 9). "Thy word have I hid in mine heart, that I might not sin against thee" (v. 11). "Open thou mine eyes, that I may behold wondrous things out of thy law" (v. 18). "I have chosen the way of truth: thy judgments have I laid before me" (v. 30). "How sweet are thy words unto my taste! Yea, sweeter than honey to my mouth!" (v. 103). "Thy word is a lamp unto my feet, and a light unto my path" (v. 105). "Thou art my hiding place and my shield: I hope in thy word" (v. 114).

## The Bread

The bread on the table in the Holy Place constituted food for the priests as they ministered daily before the Lord. It pointed ahead to the Lord Jesus Christ, who is the Bread of Life. In showing His superiority to the manna which came down from heaven, Jesus said, "I am the bread of life: he that cometh to me shall never hunger; and he that believeth on me shall never thirst" (John 6:35). In the same discourse, Jesus repeated the statement: "I am that bread of life" (v. 48). He also said, "I am the living bread which came down from heaven: if any man eat of this bread, he shall live for ever: and the bread that I will give is my flesh, which I will give for the life of the world" (v. 51).

The importance of the words of Jesus in giving sustenance for spiritual life is seen in verse 63: "It is the spirit that quickeneth; the flesh profiteth nothing: the words that I speak unto you, they are spirit, and they are life." So when Christ spoke about eating His flesh, he was not talking about His actual flesh but about believing in what He had said. His words were life-giving. Now we have the written Word which presents to us the living Word. The sustaining food of the believer is the Word of God, both the living Word (Jesus Christ) and the written Word (the Bible).

The bread in the tabernacle was replaced regularly, which indicates to us the need of coming to the Word of God each day for a fresh portion. We are not to rely on what we have gained from the Word in previous days, even as we do not rely physically on what we have eaten in previous days. A person may have had a wonderful devotional time yesterday, but that does not suffice for today. We need to keep coming to the Word of God to learn more of Christ and to assimilate the knowledge freshly each day.

In his Christian growth and experience, the Apostle Paul never considered himself to have completely attained. He said, "Not as though I had already attained, either were already perfect: but I follow after, if that I may apprehend that for which also I am apprehended of Christ Jesus. Brethren, I count not myself to have apprehended: but this one thing I do, forgetting those things which are behind, and reaching forth unto those things which are before, I press toward the mark for the prize of the high calling of God in Christ Jesus" (Phil. 3:12-14).

I think one of the best illustrations of the need for a daily devotional time is seen in Israel's wilderness experience as the people gathered manna each day. Jesus Himself drew an analogy between feeding on Him and the Old Testament manna (see John 6). When God announced that He would give manna to the Israelites, He told Moses, "In the morning, then ye shall see the glory of the Lord" (Ex. 16:7). The manna came in the morning and was to be gathered in the morning. To me, this is a beautiful picture of the need to take time early in the morning to behold the glory of God before the day's work begins.

Concerning the manna, God instructed the Israelites: "Gather of it every man according to his eating" (v. 16). Each one was to gather what he needed.

It was not possible to gather enough manna to last for the next day, for it would spoil (see v. 20). There is an important lesson here: We need to glean something from God's Word each day, not relying on the past or endeavoring to make it suffice for tomorrow.

### Ready to Serve

There were no chairs in the Holy Place of the tabernacle. This meant that the priests ate bread while they were standing.

This is a reminder of the way the Israelites ate the Passover lamb and the unleavened bread on the night they were delivered from Egypt. God told them, "Thus shall ye eat it; with your loins girded, your shoes on your feet, and your staff in your hand; and ye shall eat it in haste: it is the Lord's passover" (Ex. 12:11). So they ate while standing, ready at any moment to receive their marching orders.

We, too, are to be ready always for the call of the Lord. We need to eat of God's Word and be strengthened, ready to be at His immediate disposal. As we eat and serve Him, we fulfill the words of Christ: "By me if any man enter in, he shall be saved, and shall go in and out, and find pasture" (John 10:9).

Are you feeding upon Him? Are you occupied with Him? What a shame it would be if, when the Lord returns, He finds us occupied with mere religious entertainment or with arguments over some pet doctrine rather than with a passion to know Him better.

Remember what Jesus said when He was only 12 years old. Mary and Joseph had taken Him to Jerusalem for the Feast of the Passover, and after the feast they started back home. They had gone a day's journey before they realized that Jesus was not with some of the relatives as they expected. They returned to Jerusalem looking for Him and found Him in the temple, listening and asking questions of the teachers of the Law. Mary said, "Son, why has thou thus dealt with us? Behold, thy father and I have sought thee sorrowing" (Luke 2:48). Jesus answered, "How is it that ye sought me? Wist ye not that I must be about my Father's business?" (v. 49). As believers, are we really concerned about doing the Father's will? Are we feeding upon the Word of God so we will get to know the Lord Jesus Christ better?

Remember, Jesus is the Bread of Life (John 6:35), and we should continuously feed on Him. Notice the words of the psalmist concerning this: "Blessed is the man that walketh not in the counsel of the ungodly, nor standeth in the way of sinners, nor sitteth in the seat of the scornful. But his delight is in the law of the Lord; and in his law doth he meditate day and night" (Ps. 1:2,3).

God's words to Joshua should be taken seriously by every believer: "This book of the law shall not depart out of thy mouth; but thou shalt meditate therein day and night, that thou mayest observe to do according to all that is written therein: for then thou shalt make thy way prosperous, and then thou shalt have good success" (Josh 1:8). Let us feed on the Word daily and put ourselves at His disposal for service.

# Chapter 11

# The Golden Lampstand

The golden lampstand, also known as the candlestick, was one of the most beautiful pieces of the tabernacle furnishings. The table of showbread stood along the north wall of the Holy Place; the golden lampstand was along the south wall.

## Construction of the Lampstand

In giving Moses directions for making the lampstand, God said, "Thou shalt make a candlestick of pure gold: of beaten work shall the candlestick be made: his shaft, and his branches, his bowls, his knops, and his flowers, shall be of the same. And six branches shall come out of the sides of it; three branches of the candlestick out of the one side, and three branches of the candlestick out of the other side" (Ex. 25:31,32).

After giving more details, God said, "And thou shalt make the seven lamps thereof: and they shall light the lamps thereof, that they may give light over against it. And the tongs thereof, and the snuffdishes thereof, shall be of pure gold. Of a talent of pure gold shall he make it, with all these vessels. And look that thou make them after their pattern, which was shewed thee in the mount" (vv. 37-40).

Notice that the lampstand was to be made of a talent of pure gold (v. 39). A talent weighed over 90 pounds. This would be about 1500 ounces, or about 1370 troy ounces, in which gold is measured. Think of what that would be worth today, considering the price per ounce of gold!

The lampstand was not to be cast in a mold; rather, it was

113

to be hammered out so that the entire lampstand was formed from the one piece of gold. It was exceedingly important that God's instructions were followed in all that was done: "Look that thou make them after their pattern, which was shewed thee in the mount" (v. 40).

Although the lampstand is referred to as a candlestick, it was not a candleholder as we commonly think of one today. Candles give light, but they are consumed in the process.

This was not the case, however, with the golden lampstand. The light was produced by burning the oil which was poured into the lampstand's special gold containers. In the Scriptures, oil is often used as a symbol of the Holy Spirit. This is especially fitting in the tabernacle because it shows us that all illumination is by the Holy Spirit.

### Typology of the Lampstand

A popular interpretation of the typology of the lampstand is that the center shaft represents Christ, who is the head of the Church, and that the six side branches represent the Church as it is united in Christ and bears light before the world. Although this interpretation at first seems to fit, there are some serious difficulties with it. For instance, there is no wood in the lampstand; therefore, it does not point to the humanity of Christ. As we have noted elsewhere, wood overlaid with gold was symbolic of the divine incarnation—that Christ was the God-Man. Since the lampstand was made of pure gold, it can represent only the deity of Christ.

As such, the lampstand represents God's presence by the Holy Spirit for illuminating all in the Holy Place of fellowship. As we will study later, the mercy seat in the Holy of Holies, also made of pure gold, reveals the mercy of Almighty God. But the purpose of the lampstand in the Holy Place was to reveal how we might have fellowship with God.

There were no windows in the tabernacle; thus, there was no natural light whatever. So the golden lampstand pointed to Christ as the only light by which the priests could fellowship with God and serve in the tabernacle. The oil in the lampstand represented the Holy Spirit, who illuminates the Word of God to the believer so that he may walk in the light of the Word.

The lack of natural light in the tabernacle also reminds us that the realm of the natural reveals nothing of the beauty of the Lord Jesus Christ. "The natural man receiveth not the things of the Spirit of God: for they are foolishness unto him: neither can he know them, because they are spiritually discerned" (I Cor. 2:14).

Those on the outside of the tabernacle saw only the drab skin covering, but those on the inside saw the beauty of the tabernacle as it was revealed by the golden lampstand. Only those who trust Christ as Saviour and thereby enter the spiritual realm are able to appreciate His beauty. Unbelievers may consider Him a great teacher with extremely high morals, but they are not able to appreciate the beauty of His deity.

Having come "inside" by receiving Christ as Saviour, Paul expressed the burning desire of his heart in these words: "That I may know him, and the power of his resurrection, and the fellowship of his sufferings, being made conformable unto his death" (Phil. 3:10). Those in the natural realm see Christ only from the world's standpoint. This results in all kinds of philosophies and speculations about Christ and the world. These, in turn, lead to false teachings such as evolution. But this is understandable, since the unsaved look only from the outside.

Some also teach that the lampstand represents believers, who are the light of the world. It is true that Jesus said, "Ye are the light of the world" (Matt. 5:14). However, this does not necessarily mean that the golden lampstand of the tabernacle pictures this.

In order for the golden lampstand to be a type of believers, who are a light to the world, it would have to be taken outside of the tabernacle and exposed to the world. But the lampstand always remained within the tabernacle, so it was not seen by the world.

So if the lampstand was to represent Christ and the Church—in union with Him, shining into the world—it would have been made of wood overlaid with gold to represent the humanity of Christ. Also, it would have been permitted to shine outside the tabernacle.

All other furniture and articles in the tabernacle were for a special purpose inside the tabernacle. Specifically, the furnishings inside the Holy Place and the Holy of Holies were for the purpose of fellowship with, and worship of, God. Even though only priests were permitted in the tabernacle building, they represent all believers today, who comprise "a royal priesthood" (I Pet. 2:9).

### Light From the Lampstand

The light from the golden lampstand shone not only on the table of showbread but also on the altar of incense, the place of intercession. It also illuminated the entire Holy Place so the priests could behold the beauty of the Lord as represented there. The light revealed the cherubim on the veil separating the Holy of Holies from the Holy Place. In effect, the cherubim guarded God's holiness and said, "Stay out," since none were permitted to enter except the high priest once a year.

So the light from the golden lampstand revealed the table of showbread, representing the Word of God, and the altar of incense, representing the place of prayer, and the cherubim on the veil to the Holy of Holies, representing guardians of the holiness of God.

The light in the Holy Place represented Jesus Christ in all of His purity. This is a vivid reminder to us of what the Bible says concerning Christ: "This then is the message which we have heard of him, and declare unto you, that God is light, and in him is no darkness at all. If we say that we have fellowship with him, and walk in darkness, we lie, and do not the truth: but if we walk in the light, as he is in the light, we have fellowship one with another, and the blood of Jesus Christ his Son cleanseth us from all sin" (I John 1:5-7).

In the tabernacle, the light represented God, through the Holy Spirit, shining in the darkness, thus producing a place of fellowship. Anything that needed to be confessed would be revealed in the place of fellowship as the light shined on the table of showbread and the altar of incense. And as is true now, it was also true then: "If we confess our sins, he is faithful and just to forgive us our sins, and to cleanse us from all unrighteousness" (1:9). The light of the Word of God is the only true light and safe guide. And the intercessory prayer life is effective only as it is accomplished in the true light of the Holy Spirit.

Notice what Jesus said of Himself as the Light of the World: "As long as I am in the world, I am the light of the world" (John 9:5). "Yet a little while is the light with you. Walk while ye have the light, lest darkness come upon you: for he that walketh in darkness knoweth not whither he goeth. While ye have light, believe in the light, that ye may be the children of light" (12:35,36).

Jesus was crucified, buried and rose again to enter the Holy Place in God's presence; thus, the Light now dwells with God.

Even though Jesus no longer dwells with us as He did with the disciples, we are not without light—His death rent the veil in two and made it possible for all believers to enter the presence of God. "Having therefore, brethren, boldness to enter into the holiest by the blood of Jesus, by a new and living way, which he hath consecrated for us, through the veil, that is to say, his flesh; and having an high priest over the house of God; let us draw near with a true heart in full assurance of faith, having our hearts sprinkled from an evil conscience, and our bodies washed with pure water" (Heb. 10:19-22).

As we walk in the light, we will have fellowship with each other as well as with God, and Jesus' blood will cleanse us from all sin (see I John 1:5-7).

Those who refuse to trust Christ as Saviour are in spiritual darkness, but those who believe in Him as Saviour walk in spiritual light.

The lampstand speaks of Christ as the believer's light in this dark interval before His return as the eternal Light in the new heaven and new earth. Although we have no actual tabernacle to come to, we have access into the true sanctuary and may walk in the light as He is in the light (v. 7).

### The Lampstand and the Holy Spirit

Notice again the composition of the lampstand: "Thou shalt make a candlestick of pure gold: of beaten work shall the candlestick be made: his shaft, and his branches, his bowls, his knops, and his flowers, shall be of the same" (Ex. 25:31).

The lampstand was not made of several separate pieces joined together but was hammered out from one chunk of pure gold. At the top of each stem was a cup into which oil was poured. Since there were seven stems, there were also seven lightholders.

Although the pure gold represents Jesus Christ in all of His deity, the seven stems remind us of the sevenfold Spirit of God with which Christ, even while on earth, was endowed. Isaiah prophesied concerning the coming of Christ and the sevenfold Spirit. The symbolism of the seven-stemmed lampstand becomes clear when we read Isaiah 11:1,2: "And there shall come forth a rod out of the stem of Jesse, and a Branch shall grow out of his roots: and the spirit of the Lord shall rest upon him, the spirit of wisdom and understanding, the spirit of counsel and might, the spirit of knowledge and of the fear of the Lord" (11:1,2).

Revelation 1:4 also speaks of the sevenfold Spirit: "John to the seven churches which are in Asia: Grace be unto you, and peace, from him which is, and which was, and which is to come; and from the seven Spirits which are before his throne."

The association of the seven-stemmed lampstand of the tabernacle with the sevenfold Spirit of God is also seen in Revelation 4:5: "Out of the throne proceeded lightnings and thunderings and voices: and there were seven lamps of fire burning before the throne, which are the seven Spirits of God." So while the seven-stemmed lampstand represents Christ to the believers as His light in a dark place, it also represents the sevenfold Spirit of God.

As we think of the lampstand representing both Jesus Christ and the Holy Spirit, we must remember that it is impossible to entirely separate the two. Romans 8:9 speaks of the Holy Spirit as "the Spirit of God" and "the Spirit of Christ": "But ye are not in the flesh, but in the Spirit, if so be that the Spirit of God dwell in you. Now if any man have not the Spirit of Christ, he is none of his."

To reveal Himself to us, Jesus Christ sent the Holy Spirit. Before Jesus ascended, He said, "Howbeit when he, the Spirit of truth, is come, he will guide you into all truth: for he shall not speak of himself; but whatsoever he shall hear, that shall he speak: and he will shew you things to come. He shall glorify me: for he shall receive of mine, and shall shew it unto you. All things that the Father hath are mine: therefore said I, that he shall take of mine, and shall shew it unto you" (John 16:13-15). Thus, we see what Christ meant when He said concerning the Holy Spirit, "He shall testify of me" (15:26).

Peter also spoke of the Holy Spirit in association with Jesus Christ: "This Jesus hath God raised up, whereof we all are witnesses. Therefore being by the right hand of God exalted, and having received of the Father the promise of the Holy Ghost, he hath shed forth this, which ye now see and hear" (Acts 2:32,33).

So the gold of the tabernacle lampstand represents the deity of the Lord Jesus Christ, and its seven stems represent the sevenfold Spirit. That Jesus Christ has the sevenfold Spirit is especially seen in Revelation 3:1. The Lord Jesus Christ Himself was speaking, and He said, "These things saith he that hath the seven Spirits of God."

It is particularly interesting to compare the seven stems of the golden lampstand to what is said in the sevenfold reference to the Holy Spirit in Isaiah 11:2.

Verse 1 gives background concerning Christ: "Then a shoot will spring from the stem of Jesse, and a branch from his roots will bear fruit" (NASB). Then notice the sevenfold reference to the Holy Spirit in verse 2: "And the Spirit of the Lord will rest on Him, the spirit of wisdom and understanding, the spirit of counsel and strength, the spirit of knowledge and the fear of the Lord" (NASB).

Isaiah 11 speaks primarily of the future kingdom; nevertheless, Jesus Christ is our High Priest now (Heb. 10:21), and believers are "a royal priesthood, an holy nation" (I Pet. 2:9). As such, we enjoy the privilege of entering the Holy Place of personal fellowship with Christ. The sevenfold Spirit rests on the glorified Christ, and believers "sit together in heavenly places in Christ Jesus" (Eph. 2:6). Our being seated with Him does not mean that we are there physically, but spiritually we enjoy the privileges of being rightly related to Jesus Christ, who is in the heavenlies, or spiritual realm.

## Seven Aspects of the Holy Spirit

Seven different aspects of the Holy Spirit are viewed in Isaiah 11:2. It is interesting to think of the seven-stemmed lampstand as each aspect is considered.

First, the Holy Spirit is referred to as "the Spirit of the Lord" (v. 2, NASB). One might think in this regard of the center stem of the lampstand, for Isaiah 11:2 says, "The Spirit of the Lord will rest on Him" (NASB).

The first pair of opposite branches may be thought of in connection with the second reference to the Spirit in Isaiah 11:2: "The spirit of wisdom and understanding." Wisdom is more than knowledge; it is the proper use of knowledge. Understanding is a distinct aspect of the Spirit's ministry, for He causes us to understand the truth.

The next pair of opposite branches could be thought of in the following reference to the Holy Spirit in Isaiah 11:2: "The spirit of counsel and might." Isaiah 9:6 lists "Counsellor" as one of the names of the incarnate Christ. The Holy Spirit gives counsel as we read the Word of God and seek His direction in applying it to our lives. The Holy Spirit also gives might in Christ, as Ephesians 6:10 says: "Be strong in the Lord, and in the power of his might." Through the Holy Spirit every believer can be mighty in Christ.

The third set of opposite branches on the golden lampstand might be thought of in connection with the last reference to the Spirit in Isaiah 11:2: "The spirit of knowledge and of the fear of the Lord." The Holy Spirit gives us knowledge of Jesus Christ. Jesus said that the Holy Spirit "shall testify of me" (John 15:26), and that "he shall take of mine, and shall shew it unto you" (16:15). The Apostle Paul's burning desire was to know Christ better (see Phil. 3:10).

The Holy Spirit gives us a new understanding of Almighty God. Job expressed it in these words: "I have heard of thee by the hearing of the ear: but now mine eye seeth thee. Wherefore I abhor myself, and repent in dust and ashes" (Job 42:5,6).

When we properly understand the Lord, we will have the proper kind of fear. It will not be fear in the sense of being afraid; rather, it will be a reverent fear. The Holy Spirit's ministry is to produce the "fear of the Lord" in us (Isa. 11:2).

During the coming Tribulation, after the Church has been caught up to be with Christ, the sevenfold Spirit will also give spiritual light and make possible judgment that is absolutely correct. During this time Christ will exercise His right as sovereign over all the world by bringing judgment on those who reject Him. He will minister judgment through the sevenfold Spirit: "Out of the throne proceeded lightnings and thunderings and voices: and there were seven lamps of fire burning before the throne, which are the seven Spirits of God" (Rev. 4:5). The Apostle John was enabled to look ahead to this time, and he said, "I beheld, and, lo, in the midst of the throne and of the four beasts, and in the midst of the elders, stood a Lamb as it had been slain, having seven horns and seven eyes, which are the seven Spirits of God sent forth into all the earth" (5:6).

### Seven Symbolic Meanings

The golden lampstand has seven distinct symbolic meanings.

First, the fact that the lampstand was made of beaten gold (Ex. 25:31) symbolizes the suffering Christ, who is now risen and glorified. The gold was beaten to shape it into the intended design. It was not melted down and poured into a mold but was beaten out of a solid piece of gold. This reminds us of the Lord Jesus Christ, who was beaten unmercifully as He willingly gave His life for us.

Gold is sometimes used as an analogy of what God wanted to produce in the believer's life. Job said, "When he hath tried me, I shall come forth as gold" (Job 23:10). Peter said, "That the trial of your faith, being much more precious than of gold that perisheth, though it be tried with fire, might be found unto praise and honor and glory at the appearing of Jesus Christ" (I Pet. 1:7).

Second, the golden lampstand was placed inside the Holy Place, not outside the tabernacle. From this we infer that Christ is hidden from the world but is revealed to the believer, who is part of the priestly family of God. The world, which views Christ from the outside, sees Him only as a great teacher or a great man, but they do not see His true preciousness. Those who receive Him as Saviour, however, have the same desire that the Apostle Paul had—to "know him, and the power of his resurrection, and the fellowship of his sufferings, being made conformable unto his death" (Phil. 3:10). Such knowledge of Christ comes only through the Holy Spirit.

The light from the golden lampstand reminds us of the Holy Spirit, who reveals the preciousness of Christ to us. And this preciousness could be seen only from within the Holy Place; none on the outside had any concept of the beauty of the light.

In our desire to know Christ better, we will recognize that we have not yet attained to the goal, but we keep pressing onward. The Apostle Paul realized this and said, "Brethren, I count not myself to have apprehended: but this one thing I do, forgetting those things which are behind, and reaching forth unto those things which are before, I press toward the mark for the prize of the high calling of God in Christ Jesus" (Phil. 3:13,14).

Third, on the golden lampstand were seven bowls filled with oil. These remind us of the sufficiency of the Spirit of Christ, who has been given to believers. From Isaiah 11:2 we have seen that the sevenfold Spirit is able to meet all our needs.

Fourth, the time in Israel's history when the golden lampstand was given to the people is significant. The Israelites were in the desert, which symbolically was dark in contrast to the light of the Promised Land where God wanted the people to be. This reminds us of Jesus Christ, who is sufficient to supply all of our needs while we are living in a dark world. We may not know which way to turn, but He is our Light, and through the Word of God He will enable us to see as we need to see.

The Bible speaks of believers as children of light in contrast to unbelievers, who are of the darkness. The Apostle Paul told believers, "But of the times and the seasons, brethren, ye have no need that I write unto you. For yourselves know perfectly that the day of the Lord so cometh as a thief in the night. For when they shall say, Peace and safety; then sudden destruction cometh upon them, as travail upon a woman with child; and they shall not escape. But ye, brethren, are not in darkness, that that day should overtake you as a thief. Ye are all the children of light, and the children of the day: we are not of the night, nor of darkness. Therefore let us not sleep, as do others; but let us watch and be sober" (I Thess. 5:1-6).

Concerning the way God guides believers in a spiritually dark world, Psalm 32:8 says, "I will instruct thee and teach thee in the way which thou shalt go: I will guide thee with mine eye."

Fifth, the seven branches of the golden lampstand holding up the seven lighted lamps foreshadow the Person of the Holy Spirit. The Spirit within the sanctuary glorifies Christ. Because every believer is now indwelt by the Holy Spirit, Paul told Christians, "Your body is a temple of the Holy Spirit who is in you" (I Cor. 6:19, NASB). Thus, the believer's body is now the sanctuary where the Holy Spirit lives to reveal Jesus Christ. Jesus promised that the Holy Spirit would "take of mine, and shew it unto you" (John 16:15), and that is what the Holy Spirit is now doing in each believer's life.

Teaching us more about Christ is the operation of the Holy Spirit directed by the glorified Son of God. The Holy Spirit ministers to us to reveal the perfections of Christ and to make Him real to us. By this ministry, the Holy Spirit endears the Lord Jesus Christ to us. Only the Holy Spirit can enable us to behold and to enjoy the excellency of Christ.

Sixth, the golden lampstand was placed opposite the table of showbread to cast light on it. There was no need for the priest to eat the bread in the dark, just as there is no need for an individual believer to read the Bible in spiritual darkness. The Holy Spirit's ministry is to illumine the Word of God to the believer so that he will understand it better.

As the light of the Holy Spirit shines on the Word of God, it will become clear to us. Hebrews 4:12 reminds us that "the word of God is quick [living], and powerful, and sharper than any twoedged sword, piercing even to the dividing asunder of soul and spirit, and of the joints and marrow, and is a discerner of the thoughts and intents of the heart."

It is necessary for the Holy Spirit to illumine the Word or

else there will be confusion and disorder. Only by the ministry of the Holy Spirit can a Christian perceive Christ as the Bread of Life to sustain him. And only by the Spirit is the believer enabled to feed on Christ and to draw from Him all that is necessary for nourishment and strength.

Seventh, the light from the lampstand was also important in connection with the golden altar of incense. Without this light, the priest could not see to minister at the prayer altar. Since the golden altar speaks of worship, supplication and intercession, the aid of the Holy Spirit is indispensable in ministry at the altar. Apart from Him, one can neither praise nor petition as he should. The New Testament says, "Likewise the Spirit also helpeth our infirmities: for we know not what we should pray for as we ought: but the Spirit itself maketh intercession for us with groanings which cannot be uttered. And he that searcheth the hearts knoweth what is the mind of the Spirit, because he maketh intercession for the saints according to the will of God" (Rom. 8:26,27).

In the present-day spiritual warfare in which the believer is engaged, he is instructed to pray in the Spirit: "Praying always with all prayer and supplication in the Spirit, and watching thereunto with all perseverance and supplication for all saints" (Eph. 6:18). One prays in the Holy Spirit by allowing the Spirit to guide what he says and even how he says it.

In my praying, I have often said, "Lord, I don't know how to pray for this, but I want Your will to be done. I won't be happy or satisfied unless Your will is completely accomplished in this matter." I believe that at such times the Holy Spirit supersedes and presents our request to the Heavenly Father, even though we do not know how we should pray about the matter.

# Chapter 12

# The Golden Altar

In examining the furniture that was in the Holy Place, it is important to remember that we are discussing the place of fellowship. This is the most important element in the believer's life—fellowship with God Himself. Satan tries to blind our eyes to this matter by doing all he can to prevent us from having fellowship with God. I am frequently reminded of a statement a missionary once wrote to me: "God is not so much concerned with what I do as with what I am, for the doing comes from the being." It is only from our fellowship with God that we become what we ought to be.

## Construction and Position of the Altar

In the Holy Place were the table of showbread and the golden lampstand, which we have already considered. Now we turn our attention to the golden altar of incense. This altar was positioned on the west side of the Holy Place, next to the veil that provided entrance into the Holy of Holies.

Concerning the altar, God told Moses, "Thou shalt make an altar to burn incense upon: of shittim wood shalt thou make it" (Ex. 30:1). God also said, "And thou shalt put it before the vail that is by the ark of the testimony, before the mercy seat that is over the testimony, where I will meet with thee. And Aaron shall burn thereon sweet incense every morning: when he dresseth the lamps, he shall burn incense upon it. And when Aaron lighteth the lamps at even, he shall burn incense upon it, a perpetual incense before the Lord throughout your generations. Ye shall offer no strange incense thereon, nor burnt-sacrifice, nor meat-offering; neither shall ye pour drink-offering thereon" (vv. 6-9).

Although the altar was made of shittim, or acacia, wood (v. 1), Moses was instructed, "Overlay it with pure gold" (v. 3). As in the other pieces of furniture made of wood overlaid with pure gold, the altar pointed to the Lord Jesus Christ in both His humanity and deity.

The altar occupied the central position in the Holy Place—it was immediately in front of the veil which was closest to the mercy seat and the ark. Since the Holy of Holies was God's dwelling place, the nearest one could be to the Holy of Holies without being in it was the altar of incense.

So, too, one cannot get closer to God than he does when he comes in prayer. And those who come to God in prayer find help. Hebrews 2:18 says, "For in that he himself hath suffered being tempted, he is able to succour [help] them that are tempted."

### The Altar and Intercession

An offering of incense was to be on the coals of fire of the golden altar continually. This was a type of Christ who, in the Father's presence, now makes continual intercessory prayer for us. "For Christ has not entered into the holy places made with hands, which are the figures of the true; but into heaven itself, now to appear in the presence of God for us" (Heb. 9:24). Because Christ continually intercedes for us, we are secure in Him. One of the greatest verses in the Bible tells us, "Wherefore he is able also to save them to the uttermost that come unto God by him, seeing he ever liveth to make intercession for them" (7:25).

The Apostle John also emphasized Christ's intercessory ministry for believers. John said, "My little children, these things write I unto you, that ye sin not. And if any man sin, we have an advocate with the Father, Jesus Christ the righteous" (I John 2:1). Thus, we can say with the Apostle Paul, "Who is he that condemneth? It is Christ that died, yea rather, that is risen again, who is even at the right hand of God, who also maketh intercession for us" (Rom. 8:34).

Whereas the brazen altar, located just inside the curtain

fence in the outer court, speaks of the Christ who died for us, the golden altar of incense, located in the Holy Place near the veil, speaks to us of Christ, who lives in heaven to intercede for us. Redemption and reconciliation took place at the brazen altar, and intercession for the redeemed took place at the golden altar of incense. Thus, the altar of incense speaks of the living, resurrected, ascended Lord and Saviour Jesus Christ.

So the tabernacle, from the brazen altar to the golden altar of incense, speaks of complete salvation in Christ. Death is seen at the brazen altar, and then there is resurrection that He might become our life and live to intercede for us as indicated by the altar of incense.

Concerning the death, burial and resurrection of Jesus Christ, the Apostle Paul said, "For I delivered unto you first of all that which I also received, how that Christ died for our sins according to the scriptures; and that he was buried, and that he rose again the third day according to the scriptures" (I Cor. 15:3,4). Think of it! Christ died for us that He might give us every spiritual blessing. This is what Paul referred to when he said, "For if, when we were enemies, we were reconciled to God by the death of his Son, much more, being reconciled, we shall be saved by his life" (Rom. 5:10).

The Lord Jesus Christ saves us from much more than just the condemnation of sin—He saves us from everything that contaminates in the daily life. This is why it can be said that He saves those "to the uttermost that come unto God by him, seeing he ever liveth to make intercession for them" (Heb. 7:25).

### The Altar and Our Prayer Life

The golden altar of incense also speaks concerning our prayer life. The altar had a continual fire and incense, but there were regular times of the day when it was specifically attended. So we are to pray continually, yet there are to be times for special prayer.

The New Testament tells us, "Pray without ceasing" (I Thess. 5:17). The original word translated "without ceasing" was used in New Testament times of a person with an incessant cough. Just as his cough was not one long drawn-

128 PORTRAITS OF CHRIST IN THE TABERNACLE

out cough, so the command to pray without ceasing does not mean that we are to pray one long drawn out prayer. Instead, it means that we are to be praying incessantly, at frequent intervals. But there are also times when we should devote special attention to a period of prayer.

Since we must rest physically, it would not be possible to pray 24 hours a day. But because Jesus Christ is God, He is able to intercede for us at any time and at all times. "He ever liveth to make intercession" (Heb. 7:25).

Even though we cannot intercede for others to the same extent that Jesus Christ does, we are personally responsible to pray for others. When the Israelites asked Samuel to pray for them because they had asked for a king against God's will, Samuel said, "God forbid that I should sin against the Lord in ceasing to pray for you" (I Sam. 12:23). Samuel considered it a sin not to pray for the Israelites. This reveals the principle that it is a sin for us not to pray for the needs of others.

The importance of intercessory prayer to the Apostle Paul is seen from what he told the believers in Colosse: "For this cause we also, since the day we heard it, do not cease to pray for you, and to desire that ye might be filled with the knowledge of his will in all wisdom and spiritual understanding" (Col. 1:9). In I Timothy 2:1-4 we are instructed to pray for everyone, especially for those in authority over us. Why is this? "That we may lead a quiet and peaceable life in all godliness and honesty" (v. 2).

One of the most remarkable intercessory prayers of the Bible is recorded in Exodus 32:10-14. Moses prayed for the people in spite of the fact that God had said, "Now therefore let me alone, that my wrath may wax hot against them, and that I may consume them: and I will make of thee a great nation" (v. 10). Moses fervently interceded for the people, and God spared them.

The importance of spending time in fellowship with the Lord is seen from an incident in the life of Mary and Martha (see Luke 10:38-42). When the Lord Jesus was in their home, Martha thought mostly about the serving and preparation while He was their guest (v. 40). But Mary spent time with the Lord. When Martha asked the Lord to instruct Mary to help her in the serving, He answered, "Martha, Martha, thou art careful and troubled about many things: but one thing is needful: and Mary hath chosen that good part, which shall not be taken away from her" (vv. 41,42). This reveals that the most important thing we can do is spend time in the presence of the Lord. He is not here physically today, but we can spend time with Him in prayer.

Abraham believed in the importance of intercessory prayer. When the Lord was going to destroy Sodom because of its wickedness, Abraham interceded for it (see Gen. 18:23-33). Abraham asked the Lord to spare the city if 50 righteous people could be found (v. 24). The Lord agreed to spare it if that number could be found. Abraham realized He might not be able to find that many, so he asked the Lord to spare it if 45 could be found (v. 28). The Lord agreed to do so. Abraham continued to intercede until he was asking the Lord to spare the city if ten righteous people could be found (v. 32). The Lord agreed to do so, but history shows that not even ten could be found. The Lord eventually destroyed the cities of Sodom and Gomorrah. But Abraham was faithful in interceding for others.

## The Believer's Highest Office

The highest office of the believer is intercessory prayer. This is more acceptable than service since God is pleased more by our worship than by our service. Service is only acceptable in relationship to our prayers and intercessions. Although service is important, the spiritual battle is won in the time of prayer rather than in the time of service.

Many shut-ins cannot actively serve; therefore, many tend to think that they have no significant place in the Lord's work. They may become jealous of the opportunities that others have to move about and do things for the Lord. However, shut-ins still have the greatest privilege and largest responsibility that all believers have—to intercede for others. This is even more important than preaching. Good preaching alone cannot win souls; it takes prayer.

The golden altar of incense speaks of Christ's intercessory prayer for believers and reveals to us the need of interceding for others. The brazen altar, the place of sacrifice, typifies our salvation; the golden altar, the place of prayer, typifies the fact that we are kept by faith in God. We are "kept by the power of God through faith unto salvation ready to be revealed in the last time" (I Pet. 1:5).

As I think of Christians who have taken the responsibility of intercessory prayer seriously, I think especially of an aunt who has been with the Lord now for many years. Although she was almost completely bedfast for 15 years, I always came away from visiting her with a new appreciation for the ministry to which God had called her—a ministry of intercession.

The importance of intercessory prayer is seen in the historical incident when Israel was locked in warfare with the Amalekites (see Ex. 17:8-16). While Joshua and the Israelites fought against the Amalekites in the valley below, Moses interceded on the mountaintop. Israel won the victory as Moses, with the help of others, prevailed in intercessory prayer.

Might each of us who knows Jesus Christ as Saviour be faithful in interceding for the needs of others.

# Chapter 13

# The Holy of Holies

Whereas the Holy Place was twice as long as it was wide, the Holy of Holies was a cube—15 feet by 15 feet by 15 feet.

## Furniture of the Holy of Holies

The Holy of Holies was God's dwelling place among His people. In this special room in the tabernacle was the ark of the covenant and the mercy seat. The ark of the covenant represented the Person of Christ, and the mercy seat of pure gold represented the throne of God in the midst of His people.

The mercy seat also revealed the mercy that God could and would extend toward a sinful people if they came by the prescribed way. This way was clearly outlined in the tabernacle because one first had to come by means of a blood sacrifice. Then the blood had to be sprinkled on the mercy seat in order to satisfy, or propitiate, the holy demands of God. Romans 3:23 says, "All have sinned, and come short of the glory of God." The following verses reveal how God was satisfied, or propitiated, concerning man's sin: "Being justified freely by his grace through the redemption that is in Christ Jesus: whom God hath set forth to be a propitiation through faith in his blood, to declare his righteousness for the remission of sins that are past, through the forbearance of God; to declare, I say, at this time his righteousness: that he might be just, and the justifier of him which believeth in Jesus" (vv. 24-26).

As the mercy seat was sprinkled with blood each year on the Day of Atonement, it typified that God had been

131

satisfied for sin through the sacrifice of Jesus Christ. Although an individual cannot satisfy God for his own sins, Jesus Christ died on the cross and became "the propitiation for our sins: and not for ours only, but also for the sins of the whole world" (I John 2:2). Because Christ fully satisfied the holy demands of God for our sin, God is completely just in extending righteousness to the one who places faith in Christ. God did not overlook sin; rather, His demands were fully satisfied in the Person of Christ.

The entrance into the Holy of Holies was carefully blocked by a curtain, or veil. This heavy curtain prevented anyone entering except the high priest, and he was able to enter only once a year on the Day of Atonement. He had to come in a carefully prescribed manner, which included a blood sacrifice. Any other person who tried to enter would die. And the high priest would also die if he tried to enter at any other time by any other means.

The other two curtains in the tabernacle—the one allowing entrance to the outer court and the one allowing entrance to the Holy Place—were curtains of invitation. They invited entrance to the place of sacrifice and to the place of fellowship. In that sense, these two curtains remind us of Christ's invitation: "Come unto me, all ye that labour and are heavy laden, and I will give you rest. Take my yoke upon you, and learn of me; for I am meek and lowly in heart: and ye shall find rest unto your souls. For my yoke is easy, and my burden is light" (Matt. 11:28-30).

In contrast to the other two curtains, the curtain, or veil, to the Holy of Holies excluded even the priests from the presence of God because free access to Him had not yet been made available through Jesus Christ. Therefore, the Holy of Holies, containing the throne of judgment and the condemning Law in the ark, was the place of the awesome presence of God.

The ark of the covenant is mentioned in Exodus 25:10-16. In this passage, we see that God clearly instructed that an ark should be made of shittim, or acacia, wood and that it should be overlaid with pure gold (vv. 10,11).

The ark was a symbol that God, through Christ, was present among His people. It was the base of His throne, and as such it was the most sacred and glorious instrument in the entire tabernacle. In fact, the tabernacle was built especially to house the ark so God could dwell among His people. The ark is the first piece of furniture mentioned after God told Moses, "Let them make me a sanctuary; that I may dwell among them" (v. 8). Thus, the ark becomes a most complete type of the Lord Jesus Christ to be found anywhere in all the Bible, for it was He who came to dwell among men (see John 1:14).

Since the ark of the covenant was made of wood overlaid with gold, both inside and outside, it speaks of the twofold nature of Christ, His humanity and His deity. However, the ark differs from the other pieces of furniture in that they pointed to some aspect of Christ's work, whereas it pointed to Christ's Person.

The brazen altar pointed to His sacrificial death. The laver typified His cleansing ministry through the Word. The table of showbread pointed to Christ as the Bread of Life. The golden lampstand spoke of Christ as the Light. The altar of incense pointed to Christ as our Intercessor.

The ark of the covenant distinctly spoke of the Person of Christ—not what He has done, but who He is. When we see who and what Jesus Christ is, we will better understand and be able to evaluate His work.

Today, too much stress is placed on what Jesus Christ does rather than on who He is. What He does is important, but who He is is far more important. This is why Paul said, "That I may know him" (Phil. 3:10). Paul did not want to just know about Christ; he wanted to know Him.

Of course, one cannot entirely divorce the Person of Christ from what He does. This is also seen in the Holy of Holies, for the ark points to the Person of Christ and the mercy seat points to His work.

### Contents of the Ark

The contents of the ark of the covenant reveal who Christ really is. It is only because of who He is that He is able to completely supply all that we need. He promises many things, and He Himself is also the provision.

For instance, Christ not only gives the believer righteousness, but He is the believer's righteousness. Thus, when God looks at those who have trusted Christ as Saviour, He sees them righteous in Christ.

Also, Christ not only gives peace, but He is the believer's peace. Not only does He give the Bread of Life, but He is the Bread of Life. Not only does He give wisdom, but He is wisdom. So we see that what Christ gives is inseparably linked to His Person.

The ark of the covenant, which speaks of Christ's Person, contained three items—the golden pot of manna, Aaron's rod that budded and the unbroken tables of Law.

Although the manna spoiled when the Israelites endeavored to keep it a day longer than they should have, God miraculously preserved a sample of the manna so it could be kept inside the ark. Exodus 16:34 says concerning the manna, "As the Lord commanded Moses, so Aaron laid it up before the Testimony, to be kept." Hebrews 9:4 refers to the ark of the covenant "wherein was the golden pot that had manna."

Since the manna had sustained the lives of the Israelites in the wilderness, it was a fitting symbol of Jesus Christ, who sustains our lives spiritually. It was a sign of Christ's faithfulness in caring for His own. When Jesus emphasized that He was the Bread of Life in John 6, He contrasted Himself with the manna that came down in the wilderness. Those who ate that manna eventually all died, but those who partake of Jesus Christ live forever. Thus, the manna in the ark of the covenant presented Christ as the great provider and sustainer of life. As we think of the fact that Christ was prophet, priest and king, we see that the golden pot of manna points to Him as the prophet. A prophet gave God's Word to others, and in John 6 Christ is presented as the Word to be eaten, even as was the manna. However, manna sustained only physical life whereas Christ as the Word sustains eternal life (vv. 58,63).

Also placed within the ark of the covenant was "Aaron's rod that budded" (Heb. 9:4). Since Aaron was a high priest, representing the people to God, this rod speaks of Christ as our High Priest, representing us before God the Father.

Numbers 17 records the incident when Aaron's authority was questioned and God caused his rod to produce blossoms as proof that His blessing was on Aaron and his descendants.

This rod, which represents Christ as our High Priest, was kept in the ark of the covenant.

The other item in the ark of the covenant was the tables of Law. Moses broke the first tables of Law when he came down from the mount and found the people in idolatry (see Ex. 32:19). However, God later told Moses, "I will write on the tables the words that were in the first tables which thou brakest, and thou shalt put them in the ark" (Deut. 10:2).

The first set of tables of stone that were broken represents man's continual breaking of the Law. Mankind is completely guilty before God because "all have sinned, and come short of the glory of God" (Rom. 3:23). Thus, the Scriptures say, "There is none righteous, no not one: there is none that understandeth, there is none that seeketh after God" (vv. 10,11).

The second set of stone tables represents Christ, who did not break the Law when He came to earth to live among men. Because He is Lord of all, these represent Him as King.

The second tables of Law set forth God's unbroken covenant in the midst of an erring people. God's righteous standards are represented in them, and because those standards could never be lowered, the tables of stone were placed in the ark as a constant reminder to the Israelites. Also, the fact that these tables were placed in the ark of the covenant in the Holy of Holies revealed that His standards are protected by God Himself.

Man's attempt to lower God's standards to match his behavior simply does not work. God's standards are prescribed in the Law, and He does not lower them for anyone. No person will be saved by keeping the Law because no one can ever keep it completely. And James 2:10 says, "For whosoever shall keep the whole law, and yet offend in one point, he is guilty of all."

So the Law represents God's perfect standard of government and judgment, and Christ Himself is this holy standard.

Hebrews 12:14 reveals that without holiness "no man shall see the Lord." It is impossible for a person to attain to the holiness of God on his own, but he can have the holiness of God imputed to him by believing in Jesus Christ as his Saviour. Thus, the new birth makes it possible for a person to receive the holiness of God and someday enter the very presence of God.

### The Mercy Seat

On top of the ark of the covenant in the Holy of Holies was the mercy seat. God told Moses, "Thou shalt make a mercy seat of pure gold" (Ex. 25:17). After specifying the size, God said, "Thou shalt make two cherubims of gold, of beaten work shalt thou make them, in the two ends of the mercy seat" (v. 18).

God also instructed, "Thou shalt put the mercy seat above upon the ark; and in the ark thou shalt put the testimony that I shall give thee. And there I will meet with thee, and I will commune with thee from above the mercy seat, from between the two cherubims which are upon the ark of the testimony, of all things which I will give thee in commandment unto the children of Israel" (vv. 21,22).

The mercy seat of pure gold represented God's throne in the midst of a sinful people. Being placed on top of the ark of the covenant, the mercy seat revealed that God could cover the ark—containing the Law which revealed His standards—and show mercy. There was a way whereby God could cover man's great sin of breaking the Law so He could be merciful to us. Although God had to remain just and righteous without lowering His standards, He could extend mercy through the sprinkling of blood on the mercy seat.

Once a year, on the Day of Atonement, the high priest entered the Holy of Holies to sprinkle the blood of a sacrifice on the mercy seat, and the sins of the people would be covered for another year. The New Testament says, "In those sacrifices there is a remembrance again made of sins every year. For it is not possible that the blood of bulls and of goats should take away sins. . . . But this man [Jesus Christ], after he had offered one sacrifice for sins for ever, sat down on the right hand of God" (Heb. 10:3,4,12).

The shedding and sprinkling of blood made it possible for God to "be just, and the justifier of him which believeth in Jesus" (Rom. 3:26). The importance and necessity of the shedding of blood was seen in Israel's experience as the nation was delivered from Egypt. Exodus 12 records that fateful night when only those who had applied the shed blood of a lamb to their doorposts were delivered from judgment. The Bible says, "Without shedding of blood is no remission [forgiveness]" (Heb. 9:22).

God can meet sinful man only on the basis of His perfect righteousness and perfect grace. These two must have a common meeting place. They found their meeting place in the cross of the Lord Jesus Christ. The offerings of the Old Testament pointed to the cross of Christ. Although the Old Testament offerings could cover sins only temporarily so God could deal with His people, they pointed to the cross and to the time when Jesus Christ would be the sacrifice to take away sins forever.

In His life, the Lord Jesus Christ magnified the Law and made it honorable by keeping it perfectly. In His death, He became the propitiation which allowed God to extend mercy to mankind. In that sense, Jesus Christ was our mercy seat, for we must come through the cross to receive His righteousness and grace. Some object to thinking there is only one way of salvation, but there is no other way, and we should rejoice that there is even one way!

The mercy seat was made from a solid piece of pure gold. It was a separate article in itself, yet it formed the lid to the ark of the covenant. There was no wood in the mercy seat, only gold. This speaks of the throne of Almighty God. It represents Jesus Christ before He took on Himself a body to live among men. We read of His preincarnate state in John 1:1,2: "In the beginning was the Word, and the Word was with God, and the Word was God. The same was in the beginning with God." The term "Word" refers to the Lord Jesus Christ, as is evident from verse 14: "And the Word was made flesh, and dwelt among us."

On each end of the mercy seat was a cherub beaten out of the same piece of pure gold. These cherubim, with their wings outstretched, overshadowed the mercy seat. They protected the untainted and absolute holiness of God as He is seen to be in the mercy seat dwelling among His sinful people.

## Meaning of the Mercy Seat

The typical meaning of the mercy seat is divinely explained in Romans 3:25. Concerning Christ, Paul said, "Whom God displayed publicly as a propitiation in His blood through faith. This was to demonstrate His righteousness, because in the forbearance of God He passed over the sins previously committed" (NASB). The Greek word translated "propitiation" in this verse is the same one translated "mercyseat" in Hebrews 9:5: "Over it [the ark of the covenant] the cherubims of glory shadowing the mercyseat." Thus, by comparing Romans 3:25 and Hebrews 9:5 we see that Jesus Christ fulfilled that to which the mercy seat pointed. He is the place of propitiation, or satisfaction, for our sins. Christ is the mercy seat because He propitiated God for our sins; thus, He is our propitiation. The Bible says, "He Himself is the propitiation for our sins; and not for ours only, but also for those of the whole world. . . . In this is love, not that we loved God, but that He loved us and sent His Son to be the propitiation for our sins" (I John 2:2; 4:10, NASB). Christ's sacrifice fully paid the penalty for sin and satisfied the holy demands of God, so it was not necessary for God to lower His standards in order to justify sinful man. Anyone who trusts Jesus Christ as Saviour receives the righteousness of Christ Himself.

There was no chair in the tabernacle because the work of the priests was never finished. From the time of the giving of the Law to the time of Christ's death on the cross the priest had to come again and again with sacrifices for the people. And even then, the sacrifice did not take away sin but only covered it for the time being.

The Book of Hebrews contrasts the work of the priest with the accomplishment of Jesus Christ: "Every priest standeth daily ministering and offering oftentimes the same sacrifices, which can never take away sins: but this man, after he had offered one sacrifice for sins for ever, sat down on the right hand of God" (Heb. 10:11,12).

The mercy seat represented the place of rest for God because it looked ahead to the time when there would be complete rest in the finished work of Christ. In this case, the word "rest" does not refer to getting relief from weariness but to a court resting its case. Hebrews 4 tells us of the rest that is in Christ Jesus. He is the end of the struggle for everyone who believes in Him and walks by faith.

Because God looked ahead to the sacrifice of Jesus Christ, He was completely satisfied with the finished work of Christ and thus rested at the mercy seat which was His throne on earth.

When God gave instructions concerning the mercy seat, He told Moses, "There I will meet with thee, and I will commune with thee from above the mercy seat, from between the two cherubims which are upon the ark of the testimony, of all things which I will give thee in commandment unto the children of Israel" (Ex. 25:22). The Bible frequently refers to the fact that God met with man above the mercy seat between the two cherubim.

Second Samuel 6:2 says, "David arose, and went with all the people that were with him from Baale of Judah, to bring up from thence the ark of God, whose name is called by the name of the Lord of hosts that dwelleth between the cherubims." Psalm 99:1 says, "The Lord reigneth; let the people tremble: he sitteth between the cherubims; let the earth be moved."

So God met man above the mercy seat between the cherubim. But it is logical to ask, How was it possible for an absolutely holy God to dwell among sinful people? It was possible only by means of the blood-sprinkled mercy seat. Leviticus 16:14,15 gives the priest instructions concerning the Day of Atonement: "He shall take of the blood of the bullock, and sprinkle it with his finger upon the mercy seat eastward; and before the mercy seat shall he sprinkle of the blood with his finger seven times. Then shall he kill the goat of the sin-offering, that is for the people, and bring his blood within the vail, and do with that blood as he did with the blood of the bullock, and sprinkle it upon the mercy seat, and before the mercy seat."

The sprinkled blood made it possible for a righteous God to dwell in the midst of an unrighteous people. It allowed Him to be just and yet also the justifier of those who came to Him by faith. How beautifully this pointed to the Lord Jesus Christ as our propitiation so that God "might be just, and the justifier of him which believeth in Jesus" (Rom. 3:26).

Christ lived a holy life, then died, making it possible for God to take a hell-deserving sinner into fellowship with Himself and yet be consistent in His holiness and justice. Christ lived to vindicate God's holiness, and He died to vindicate God's justice and judgment on sin.

God could not exercise mercy at the expense of His justice and judgment. His holy character was involved, but in Christ (a fulfillment of the mercy seat) God's avenging holiness was fully satisfied by the shedding of blood on the cross. Justice had received full payment.

By His life, Jesus Christ magnified the Law and made it honorable. In this, He was a fulfillment of Isaiah 42:21: "The Lord is well pleased for his righteousness' sake; he will magnify the law, and make it honorable."

The Lord Jesus Christ lived a perfect life, and by His death all the divine perfections were established. God's love, grace and mercy were all manifested at Calvary as nowhere else. Because of what Christ accomplished on the cross, Paul said, "Therefore we conclude that a man is justified by faith without the deeds of the law. . . . Do we then make void the law through faith? God forbid: yea, we establish the law" (Rom. 3:28,31). We establish the Law in the sense that we acknowledge our guilt and recognize that we justly deserve condemnation, but we are delivered from condemnation by trusting Jesus Christ as our substitute for sin.

In connection with establishing the Law, notice what Christ Himself said: "Think not that I am come to destroy the law, or the prophets: I am not come to destroy, but to fulfil. For verily I say unto you, Till heaven and earth pass, one jot or one tittle shall in no wise pass from the law, till all be fulfilled" (Matt. 5:17,18).

The holiness, justice and righteousness of Christ were also established as He gave Himself on the cross for the sin of the world. He was the fulfillment of the Old Testament mercy seat because only by means of the blood shed on the cross can the sinner find mercy.

## Blessings of the Mercy Seat

Consider now some of the special blessings of the mercy seat. Remember, it was the place where God communicated with man. It is interesting to trace through the Bible the different means God used to communicate with man.

In the Garden of Eden, there was direct communication, but then sin broke fellowship, and God had to drive man out of the garden. God communicated to the prophets of old through dreams and visions. Then Jesus Christ Himself came to earth to reveal God to man. During Old Testament times, however, God communicated primarily by means of the tabernacle, especially from over the mercy seat between the cherubim.

One special blessing of the mercy seat was the fact that it covered the ark and thus overshadowed the Law which was inside. This was God's way of revealing another aspect about His Person. The Law revealed His righteousness and demanded death of the one who violated it.

Galatians 3:10 reveals the judgment of God that was on every violator of the Law: "For as many as are of the works of the law are under the curse: for it is written, Cursed is every one that continueth not in all things which are written in the book of the law to do them." And this is still true today. Anyone who seeks to become right with God through the keeping of the Law must keep it perfectly, and of course, no one except the Lord Jesus Christ has ever been able to do that.

Because Jesus Christ was able to perfectly keep the Law, He might have exercised judgment on all of us who are not able to do so. Instead, He came to deliver us from the curse of the Law by fulfilling it Himself and then offering Himself as a sacrifice for our sin. On the cross, He received the penalty which was due us, according to the Law. Thus, the storm of God's wrath was spent on Him so that the Law can no longer touch anyone who flees to Him, by faith, for refuge.

By parallel, the mercy seat covered the Law within the ark just as Christ covered the Law in our regard. This enables us to see how the mercy seat represented the Lord Jesus Christ.

As the mercy seat covered the Law and the blood sprinkled on the mercy seat covered sin, so Jesus Christ completely fulfilled the Law and then died on the cross to deliver us from the penalty of the Law. Jesus Christ fulfilled the Law, first in His life and then in His death. No one could point a finger at Him and say, "You did not fulfill the Law." In His death, He fulfilled it by accepting the penalty of death for all men, who were unable to meet the demands of the Law.

The Bible says, "Christ hath redeemed us from the curse of the law, being made a curse for us: for it is written, Cursed is every one that hangeth on a tree" (3:13). The weakness of the Law is seen in another passage: "For what the law could not do, in that it was weak through the flesh, God sending his own Son in the likeness of sinful flesh, and for sin, condemned sin in the flesh" (Rom. 8:3). Nothing is wrong with the Law itself, but because of the weakness of human nature no one could keep it.

But the demands of the Law have to be met; they cannot be bypassed. This is why the mercy seat had to be sprinkled with blood, indicating man had come by God's prescribed way. Even though we cannot keep the Law perfectly, Jesus Christ did, and we come by means of the shed blood when we receive Him as our Saviour.

The Old Testament provides an illustration of what happens when the mercy seat is removed from the ark so that the Law is uncovered. In Israel's military skirmishes the ark had been taken by the Philistines. Because they were uneasy about having it in their presence, the Philistines hitched two milk cows to it. They knew it would be of the Lord if the cows took the ark toward Israel, and this is precisely what they did. The account is given in I Samuel 6 of how the ark was brought to a wheat field where harvesting was in process. The people erred in that they looked into the ark of God, which meant the mercy seat was removed, and the holy standards of the Law were fully exposed.

The judgment that falls when the Law is exposed apart from the mercy of God is seen from verses 19,20: "He smote the men of Beth-shemesh, because they had looked into the ark of the Lord, even he smote of the people fifty thousand and threescore and ten men: and the people lamented, because the Lord had smitten many of the people with a great slaughter. And the men of Beth-shemesh said, Who is able to stand before this holy Lord God? And to whom shall he go up from us?" We, too, need to realize that we cannot stand before the Law apart from the mercy of God; our only hope is to acknowledge our sinful condition and trust in Jesus Christ as our personal Saviour.

Another special blessing of the mercy seat was that it was the place where God met the sinner through a representative. This representative was the high priest, who entered the Holy of Holies once a year on the Day of Atonement to sprinkle blood on the mercy seat and thus atone for the sin of the people (see Lev. 16:14-16).

Today, Christ is our High Priest, for He has made the way into the Holy of Holies available to all who come by means of His shed blood. "Having therefore, brethren, boldness to enter into the holiest by the blood of Jesus, by a new and living way, which he hath consecrated for us, through the veil, that is to say, his flesh" (Heb. 10:19,20).

No one could see the high priest enter the Holy of Holies and approach the mercy seat with blood, but by faith they followed him there. We, too, cannot see the throne of mercy and grace with our physical eyes, but through the eyes of faith we may enter the Holy of Holies by means of Christ's shed blood for our sin.

Another special blessing of the mercy seat was that it became the place of spiritual communion. God instructed Moses, "Thou shalt put the mercy seat above upon the ark; and in the ark thou shalt put the testimony that I shall give thee. And there I will meet with thee, and I will commune with thee from above the mercy seat, from between the two cherubims which are upon the ark of the testimony, of all things which I will give thee in commandment unto the children of Israel" (Ex. 25:21,22).

An example of how God communed with man from the mercy seat is seen in Numbers 7:89: "When Moses was gone into the tabernacle of the congregation to speak with him, then he heard the voice of one speaking unto him from off the mercy seat that was upon the ark of testimony, from between the two cherubims: and he spake unto him." Although Moses was probably not allowed into the Holy of Holies, he could commune with God as the other priests did from the other side of the curtain in the Holy Place.

Through the Lord Jesus Christ, the believer is also brought into the Holy of Holies, the place of blessing in the presence of God. The Lord Jesus communes and intercedes for us from the true Holy of Holies. "Seeing then that we have a great high priest, that is passed into the heavens, Jesus the Son of God, let us hold fast our profession. For we have not an high priest which cannot be touched with the feeling of our infirmities; but was in all points tempted like as we are, yet without sin. Let us therefore come boldly unto the throne of grace, that we may obtain mercy, and find grace to help in time of need" (Heb. 4:14-16). Jesus Christ is now at the right hand of the Father, and He "is able also to save them to the uttermost that come unto God by him, seeing he ever liveth to make intercession for them" (7:25).

Since Jesus Christ is on the mercy seat on the throne of God, we need to come boldly into His presence to commune with Him there. If we have trusted Jesus Christ as Saviour, we have been reconciled to God, so let us draw near the throne of grace in full assurance and faith.

Chapter 14

# The Veil

Having considered what was on the inside of the Holy of Holies—the ark of the covenant and the mercy seat—we now focus special attention on the veil that covered the entrance to the Holy of Holies.

## Appearance of the Veil

When giving instructions to Moses concerning the tabernacle, God said, "Thou shalt make a vail of blue, and purple, and scarlet, and fine twined linen of cunning work: with cherubims shall it be made: and thou shalt hang it upon four pillars of shittim wood overlaid with gold: their hooks shall be of gold, upon the four sockets of silver. And thou shalt hang up the vail under the taches, that thou mayest bring in thither within the vail the ark of the testimony: and the vail shall divide unto you between the holy place and the most holy" (Ex. 26:31-33).

Since the veil was made of fine linen, it represented the complete holiness and righteousness of Christ Himself. On the veil were cherubim in three colors—blue, purple and scarlet—all pointing to Jesus Christ, the incarnate One, who is the only way to the Father. Jesus said, "I am the way, the truth, and the life: no man cometh unto the Father, but by me" (John 14:6).

Cherubim were not on the curtains of the entrance to the outer court or of the entrance to the Holy Place. They were only on the curtain of entrance to the Holy of Holies. They were also on the inner roof of the tabernacle; thus, they could be seen by the priests ministering in the Holy Place.

145

As indicated previously, cherubim were symbolic of protecting the holiness of God. They were placed on the east side of the Garden of Eden "to keep the way of the tree of life" (Gen. 3:24). And cherubim were also on the mercy seat where God communed with man (see Ex. 25:22).

On the veil of entrance to the Holy of Holies, the cherubim represented protection of the inner room where God's throne was.

The veil shut out everyone from the Holy of Holies except the high priest, who was allowed to enter only once a year on the Day of Atonement. Hebrews 10:20 speaks of the veil as being Christ's "flesh," by which He made access to God available to all.

The veil covering the entrance to the Holy of Holies was both the way and the barrier to the interior where the ark of the covenant and the mercy seat were found. It was the way for the high priest to enter once a year, but it was a barrier to all others at all times.

The reason for this barrier concerns the significance of the ark and its contents. The ark represented the God-Man, Jesus Christ, for it was made of wood overlaid with pure gold. Inside the ark were the two stone tablets of the Law which testified to the unbroken standards of God's holiness. To meet God, a person had to keep these standards perfectly from birth to death, which was accomplished only by the Lord Jesus Christ. But the ark was covered with a mercy seat of pure gold, revealing that God would be merciful if man came by a prescribed way.

The mercy seat in the Holy of Holies was God's throne on earth during Old Testament times as He dwelt among sinful men. But even as He did, the cherubim over the mercy seat as well as the cherubim on the veil to the Holy of Holies indicated that His holiness was guarded and that His standards were lowered in no way.

The veil covering the entrance to the Holy of Holies kept everyone from the immediate presence of God except the high priest. However, when Christ was crucified, this veil, then in the temple, was torn in two. "Jesus, when he had cried again with a loud voice, yielded up the ghost. And, behold, the veil of the temple was rent in twain from the top to the bottom; and the earth did quake, and the rocks rent"

(Matt. 27:50,51). Hebrews 10:20 reveals that the veil was a type of the body of Jesus: "By a new and living way, which he hath consecrated for us, through the veil, that is to say, his flesh."

## Significance of the Veil

As we have already seen, the purpose of the veil's covering the entrance to the Holy of Holies was to keep out everyone except the high priest. No one else could enter, and even he could enter only once a year. If anyone else entered or if the high priest tried to enter at another time, it meant certain death. "The Lord said unto Moses, Speak unto Aaron thy brother, that he come not at all times into the holy place within the vail before the mercy seat, which is upon the ark; that he die not: for I will appear in the cloud upon the mercy seat" (Lev. 16:2). Behind this veil was the throne of God, and in the ark was the Law which condemned the sinner before God. This is why it was so important that no one enter except by God's prescribed way.

Although the curtains across the entrances to the outer court and the Holy Place invited people to enter, the curtain to the Holy of Holies was designed to forbid entry. The curtain to the outer court allowed entrance by means of sacrifice, and the curtain to the Holy Place allowed entrance to the place of fellowship. However, the curtain to the Holy of Holies, the place of worship, kept all out except the high priest until the way was made open through the Lord Jesus Christ. As the priests ministered within the Holy Place, they were constantly made aware of the holiness of God by viewing the cherubim on the inner roof as well as on the veil covering the Holy of Holies.

The key to understanding the significance of the veil is to recognize that it points to the body of the Lord Jesus Christ. As such, the veil represents Christ in His perfect, sinless humanity as He took on Himself a human body (see John 1:14). He thereby represented to mankind the absolute, perfect holiness of God. Since Jesus Christ was a perfect being, He kept the Law of God in every detail.

Notice two particular truths concerning Jesus Christ as He lived on earth. First, He revealed God's perfect holiness.

He was without sin (I John 3:5); no one could point a finger of blame at Him. Thus, He was able to say, "He that hath seen me hath seen the Father" (John 14:9). The Lord Jesus Christ totally represented the Father in all of His holiness.

Second, as He walked on earth, the Lord Jesus Christ revealed the standard man must attain if he expects to meet God. Only the person who is perfectly sinless can ever expect to approach God, and no one except the Lord Jesus Christ is perfectly sinless. At first it seems hopeless for any to expect to stand before God, but the Good News is that Jesus Christ has paid the penalty of sin for us so that we can stand before God by faith in Jesus Christ. "When the fulness of the time was come, God sent forth his Son, made of a woman, made under the law, to redeem them that were under the law, that we might receive the adoption of sons" (Gal. 4:4,5).

The perfection of the God-Man only served to emphasize the imperfections of fallen man. Thus, Jesus Christ made the awful distance between an absolutely holy God and a totally depraved human being even more evident. It is interesting to notice the response of man—even in Old Testament times—when he saw God in all of His holiness. This caused Isaiah to say, "Woe is me! for I am undone; because I am a man of unclean lips, and I dwell in the midst of a people of unclean lips: for mine eyes have seen the King, the Lord of hosts" (Isa. 6:5). Job said, "I abhor myself, and repent in dust and ashes" (Job 42:6).

People may admire the character and teachings of Christ in His earthly life, but the primary object of His life was to reveal God's holiness and to show that man is forever excluded from God unless he comes through Christ. This was the same purpose of the veil across the entrance to the Holy of Holies; it excluded man unless he came in God's prescribed way. The cherubim on the curtain even indicated that man should stay away from the holiness of God, just as the cherubim guarded the tree of life in the Garden of Eden (Gen. 3:24).

So the Lord Jesus Christ, while He was on earth, revealed the impossibility of any approach to God unless sin could be paid for and the person could become as holy as Christ. The Bible says, "There is none righteous, no not one: there is none that understandeth, there is none that seeketh after

God. . . . For all have sinned, and come short of the glory of God" (Rom. 3:10,11,23).

It was not the beauty of the veil that made entrance possible just as it was not the beauty of Christ's earthly life that makes salvation possible. There had to be the sprinkling of the atoning blood in Old Testament times, which pointed forward to the necessity of the Lord Jesus Christ's shedding His blood on the cross. No one is saved from condemnation by endeavoring to imitate the life of Christ or by attempting to keep the Law. There has to be the shedding of blood and its application to the individual.

Those who put their hope in the Law need to be aware of Romans 3:19,20: "Now we know that what things soever the law saith, it saith to them who are under the law: that every mouth may be stopped, and all the world may become guilty before God. Therefore by the deeds of the law there shall no flesh be justified in his sight: for by the law is the knowledge of sin."

The veil of the Holy of Holies was upheld by "four pillars of shittim wood overlaid with gold" (Ex. 26:32). These four pillars are a reminder of the four Gospel accounts concerning the life and ministry of the Lord Jesus Christ.

Whereas the veil displayed the holy beauty of the God-Man, the four pillars pointed to the four Gospels that revealed and upheld the glories of this sinless Person.

### The Torn Veil

The Bible gives special attention to the tearing of the veil in the temple at Christ's death. This made access into the presence of God available to all. It is not certain how thick the veil of the tabernacle was, although it may have been as much as four inches thick. Stories have circulated about its thickness. Some have even suggested that two teams of oxen pulling in opposite directions could not tear it.

As we have seen, the purpose of the veil was to reveal God's holiness and man's unholiness. Jesus lived on earth for about 33 years revealing the same truths. And after revealing God's perfect character, the Lord Jesus Christ presented Himself as the sacrifice for sins to suffer the penalty of the

Law for all mankind. This provided the only possible way for sinful man to enter the presence of God.

Notice what happened to the veil when Christ finished His work of redemption on the cross. "The veil of the temple was rent in twain from the top to the bottom" (Matt. 27:51). This was God's work, not man's. Christ completely satisfied the standards of God and, in so doing, God was propitiated and man was completely reconciled. Thus, it was possible for God to be "just, and the justifier of him which believeth in Jesus" (Rom. 3:26). Hebrews 1:3 says concerning Christ, "When he had by himself purged our sins, sat down at the right hand of the Majesty on high." Now He calls on us to believe in Him as personal Saviour and to acknowledge Him before others (see Rom. 10:9,10). Sin was put away in the sacrifice of Christ, and the perfect righteousness of God is available to all who believe. Thus, man has access to God.

Notice that at the crucifixion the veil was torn in two (Matt. 27:51); it was not just a little hole allowing one to see inside the Holy of Holies. That which was once a barrier became the gateway. The veil was torn in two when Christ died because it was then that His body was broken and torn for us. The Lord Jesus Christ "was delivered for our offences, and was raised again for our justification" (Rom. 4:25). God now looks on every believer in Christ Jesus as being as perfect as Christ Himself. Why? It is because God sees us only as we are in Christ; the sin question has been forever settled, and we are clothed in the perfect righteousness of Christ.

Although the sacrifices of the Old Testament could not take away sin, Jesus Christ did so by His death on the cross. "For it is not possible that the blood of bulls and of goats should take away sins. Wherefore when he cometh into the world, he saith, Sacrifice and offering thou wouldest not, but a body hast thou prepared me. . . . By the which [God's] will we are sanctified through the offering of the body of Jesus Christ once for all. . . . For by one offering he hath perfected for ever them that are sanctified" (Heb. 10:4,5,10,14).

Thus, we have seen why the veil of the Holy of Holies pointed to Jesus Christ: By giving His body on the cross, He made access into the presence of God available to all. "Having therefore, brethren, boldness to enter into the holiest by the blood of Jesus, by a new and living way, which he hath consecrated for us, through the veil, that is to say, his flesh" (10:19,20).

Although the sacrifices in the Old Testament had to be offered over and over again, "this man, after he had offered one sacrifice for sins for ever, sat down on the right hand of God" (10:12). How wonderful to realize that Jesus Christ accomplished our redemption by being the sacrifice for sins and paying the penalty once for all. Thus, we are invited to "come boldly unto the throne of grace, that we may obtain mercy, and find grace to help in time of need" (4:16).

Even though Jesus Christ has made the way available to all who come by faith, many still refuse Him as the one way of salvation. But the Bible is clear. Even though man devises his own way of salvation, there is no other way except through Christ. "Neither is there salvation in any other: for there is none other name under heaven given among men, whereby we must be saved" (Acts 4:12). Just as the Israelites experienced death if they tried to enter the Holy of Holies in a way other than God's prescribed way, all experience spiritual death unless they come to God through Jesus Christ. "The wages of sin is death" (Rom. 6:23).

Any gospel that says salvation is possible through something or someone other than Jesus Christ is a false gospel. The Apostle Paul preached salvation only through Jesus Christ, and he said, "If any man preach any other gospel unto you than that ye have received, let him be accursed" (Gal. 1:9).

Tradition tells us that the priests tried to mend the veil after it was torn in two when Christ died on the cross. So, also, men have been devising their own ways of salvation rather than coming to Christ by faith. But their attempts are as useless as the priests' attempt to mend the veil. All who refuse to come to Christ will be eternally condemned.

Man's attempts to come by some way other than by Jesus Christ reveals the total depravity of mankind. Man will not humble himself and admit his sinfulness. As a result he shuts himself out of heaven and the presence of God.

Concerning salvation, Titus 3:5 says, "Not by works of righteousness which we have done, but according to his mercy he saved us, by the washing of regeneration, and renewing of the Holy Ghost." Romans 4:5 says, "But to him that worketh not, but believeth on him that justifieth the ungodly, his faith is counted for righteousness."

Have you acknowledged your sinful condition and realized that your only hope is Jesus Christ, who paid the penalty of sin for you? Is so, have you placed your trust in Jesus Christ as your personal Saviour? If not, do so before it is eternally too late.

"This is the record, that God hath given to us eternal life, and this life is in his Son. He that hath the Son hath life; and he that hath not the Son of God hath not life" (I John 5:11,12).

# Chapter 15

# A Pattern for the Devotional Time

With the truths of God's Word concerning the tabernacle fresh in our minds, it is good to specifically remind ourselves of the distinctive difference in the way we are able to approach God today.

I suggest you think of this in relation to the devotional time that each believer should have with God. This is to be a period of time in which the believer shuts the world out and shuts himself in to God to read and meditate on the Word and to bring his petitions before God. Many Christians have a tremendous struggle finding time to spend alone with God, but let me urge you to do everything you can to arrange your priorities so you will be able to spend time with God each day.

If it has not been your custom to have a personal devotional time, may I suggest that you set aside 15 minutes a day for this purpose. Arrange your schedule to be sure you get this time to be alone with God. You may have to cut some things out of your schedule to make room for a devotional time. If you are serious about wanting a devotional time but have difficulty fitting it into your schedule, let me suggest that you make a record of everything that you do in an average day. Number each activity according to its importance. Be sure to allow plenty of time for the family, for meals and for sleep. The activities at the bottom of the list, which are the least important, should be eliminated to make room for a devotional time in your daily schedule. This may mean that you will have to give up doing some things you enjoy, or it may mean giving up things that others think you should do. But you must determine on your own before God what you will exclude from your schedule to allow time for a devotional period.

You will discover that the truths we have learned about the tabernacle serve as a pattern for devotions. For instance, as the Israelite of the Old Testament entered the gate at the eastern end of the outer court, he shut out the world. So, too, the believer who approaches God during his devotional time shuts out the world as he finds a quiet place to be alone with God. As much as possible, you will find it helpful to select a place where you can come each day for the devotional time. Then you will not have to wonder about a place but can concentrate on how you will spend this important time with God. It should be a quiet place so the world is shut out as you come before God.

Jesus said, "I am the door: by me if any man enter in, he shall be saved, and shall go in and out, and find pasture" (John 10:9). As the believer enters the privacy of his devotional place and time, he is entering as God intends that he should do.

## The Outer Court

Just inside the gate of the outer court was the brazen altar where the sacrifice was offered for sin. In the devotional time, the believer today can thank the Lord that one sacrifice for sin has been offered forever. Referring to the Lord Jesus Christ, Hebrews 10:12 says, "This man, after he had offered one sacrifice for sins for ever, sat down on the right hand of God."

In his devotional time, the believer should thank God that He has been satisfied, or propitiated, for sin by the sacrifice of the Lord Jesus Christ. And having trusted Christ as Saviour, the believer has died with Christ and to the things of the world. Romans 6 is a key passage of Scripture revealing that the believer has died with Christ and has been raised to newness of life. It is an excellent passage of Scripture to use in the devotional time to remind the believer of all that he has in Jesus Christ.

In the tabernacle, as one moved from the brazen altar toward the Holy Place, he came next to the laver. The laver was to be used for cleansing. So, too, after thanking God that the penalty of his sins has been paid, the believer should examine his life to see if an individual sin, which has been committed since salvation, needs to be confessed. The Holy Spirit uses the Word of God to bring conviction of sin, so it is often as the believer reads the Bible that he sees the need of cleansing.

Christ's word brings cleansing, as we are told in John 15:3: "Now ye are clean through the word which I have spoken unto you." The Church, that is, believers making up the body of Christ, is sanctified by "the washing of water by the word" (Eph. 5:26). The psalmist said, "Wherewithal shall a young man cleanse his way? By taking heed thereto according to thy word. . . . Thy word have I hid in mine heart, that I might not sin against thee" (Ps. 119:9,11).

God's Word promises, "If we confess our sins, he is faithful and just to forgive us our sins, and to cleanse us from all unrighteousness" (I John 1:9). Upon confessing any sin that has come to our attention, we should thank God for the forgiveness He has promised. How tragic it is that some believers confess their sin but fail to claim the promise of God that He forgives when we confess.

It is true that none of us deserve forgiveness, but God forgives us on the basis of what Jesus Christ accomplished on the cross. So the forgiveness of sin does not depend on us but on what the Lord Jesus Christ did for us. So thinking of the laver, we can thank God in our devotional time for the cleansing that results when we confess our sins.

### The Holy Place

From the laver, the priest in the Old Testament tabernacle passed through a curtain into the Holy Place. There he was shut in to God. So also, in our devotional time we are shut in to God, having thanked Him for paying the penalty of our sins and for cleansing us from daily sin on the basis of the Word and our confession. At the gate of the outer court the world was shut out, but in the Holy Place the emphasis was on the priest being shut in to God. Both aspects are true of the devotional time today. The world is shut out as we come apart to spend time alone with God, and it also serves as that time when we are shut in to God. You will be thrilled with the devotional time more and more as you experience the blessing of shutting out the world and of being shut in with God.

On entering the Holy Place, the priest saw on his left the golden lampstand that provided light in the tabernacle enclosure. We have seen in our previous study that the lampstand was symbolic of the Holy Spirit, who reveals the Person of Christ to us. The Lord Jesus Christ said concerning the Holy Spirit: "He shall glorify me: for he shall receive of mine, and shall shew it unto you" (John 16:14). Thus, in the devotional time the believer today can thank God for the Holy Spirit who reveals to us truths concerning Jesus Christ.

In the Holy Place, the lampstand clearly revealed the table of showbread that sat against the opposite wall. Jesus referred to Himself as the Bread of Life (see John 6:35,48). Jesus Christ is the Living Word of God (John 1:1), and the Bible is the written Word. So we feed on the Bread of Life, who is Jesus Christ, by feeding on the written Word. And it is the Holy Spirit's ministry to reveal to us truths from the Scriptures about the Person and work of Christ which enable us to know Christ more intimately. A very important part of our devotional time should be spent meditating on His Word.

Also within the Holy Place was the altar of incense sitting just in front of the veil leading into the Holy of Holies. The altar of incense was the place of prayer, especially of interceding for others. In his devotional time, the believer prays for himself concerning individual sin at the place of cleansing, the laver. But at the altar of incense he prays for the needs of others. This simply serves as a reminder that we need to be right with God personally before we engage in the important task of praying for others.

### The Holy of Holies

In Old Testament times the veil to the Holy of Holies kept the priests from entering, except for the high priest who was able to enter once a year on the Day of Atonement. Today, however, we can visualize looking directly into the Holy of Holies because the veil has been torn in two. The Bible tells us of this in Hebrews 10:19,20: "Having therefore, brethren, boldness to enter into the holiest by the blood of Jesus, by a new and living way, which he hath consecrated for us, through the veil, that is to say, his flesh." Matthew 27:51 tells of the veil of the temple being torn in two from top to bottom when Christ finished His work of redemption on the cross. God has been fully satisfied for the penalty of sin, and any person can enter the very presence of God by means of the shed blood of Jesus Christ.

So in the devotional time we have proceeded from where we were in the world (although not of it) to the very presence of God. After interceding for others, we leave this special place at the close of the devotional time to again enter the activities of life as a radiant witness for Jesus Christ. Jesus said, "I am the door: by me if any man enter in, he shall be saved, and shall go in and out, and find pasture" (John 10:9). The believer entered into the devotional time to worship God and to pray for the needs of others. Only then is he ready to go out to be a witness for Christ.

As the believer goes out from his devotional time he can be confident that Jesus Christ goes before him. Jesus likened Himself to a good shepherd, of whom He said, "When he putteth forth his own sheep, he goeth before them, and the sheep follow him: for they know his voice" (10:4). Jesus goes before, but it is tremendously important for the believer to follow wherever He leads. Jesus said, "If any man will come after me, let him deny himself, and take up his cross daily, and follow me" (Luke 9:23).

As the believer leaves the devotional time he can think of the Old Testament priest leaving the tabernacle. As the believer passes the table of showbread he can thank God for the written Word which he has been allowed to feed on, and as he passes the lampstand he can thank God for the Holy Spirit, who has been given to help each one understand the things of God. Passing by the laver, the believer can remind himself that in himself he is nothing but in Christ he is everything. As he passes by the brazen altar he can remind himself that he has died with Christ and has died to the things of the world. He is then to be a vibrant witness for Jesus Christ. The believer can say with the Apostle Paul, "Thanks be unto God, which always causeth us to triumph in

Christ" (II Cor. 2:14); and "I can do all things through Christ which strengtheneth me" (Phil. 4:13).

So think of the tabernacle as a pattern for your devotional time with the Lord. Although you may spend only a few minutes at first, I encourage you to be as regular as possible in your devotional time. You will soon discover that you will want more minutes for this wonderful period when you shut out the world and shut yourself in to God to have your own heart cleansed as you confess your sin, to be strengthened spiritually as you read and meditate on the Bible, and to bring the needs of others before the throne of grace. As you faithfully spend time with God and His Word and apply it to your daily life, you will mature spiritually and will be used to spiritually enrich many lives.